SILENT APPROACH

SILENT APPROACH

The Operations of The Glider Pilot Regiment in World War II

John Hemmings, M.C.

The Book Guild Ltd
Sussex, England

The Book Guild Ltd
25 High Street,
Lewes, Sussex

First published 1999

Set in Times

Typesetting by Wordset,
Lewes, East Sussex

Printed in Great Britain by
Bookcraft (Bath) Ltd.Avon

A catalogue record for this book is
available from the British Library

ISBN 1 85776 377 7

CONTENTS

To all former pilots of
The Glider Pilot Regiment

Also to my dear wife Lilyan for all her love, care and encouragement through the years. My thanks also to my son, John, for his help and suggestions during the preparation of this book.

ACKNOWLEDGEMENTS

I am grateful to all those who have helped to compile this book. So many former pilots of The Glider Pilot Regiment, and others, answered letters and my appeals in the press and on the radio; to each of them I owe my thanks.

My thanks also to Betsy Ho and Valentine Fung, who shared the typing of the manuscript.

That Major General His Grace The Duke of Norfolk has written the Foreword gives me great pleasure.

Unlike previous works about The Glider Pilot Regiment this book does not attempt a definitive history, nor does it attempt a detached account of the overall strategy of individual battles in which the regiment took part. Instead it relates the experiences of some of the surviving pilots who flew men, arms and equipment to landing zones behind enemy lines and then fought with the Allied forces, side by side.

Unless you stake your life you cannot win it.

Anon

FOREWORD

by
Major General His Grace The Duke of Norfolk,
KG,GCVO, CB, CBE, MC

During the Second World War British glider pilots, and the regiment that embodied them, earned the greatest respect of other British Regiments, their Allies and the enemy alike, for their superlative skills as pilots and as soldiers on the ground.

It was an order from Winston Churchill, on the 22 June 1940, which led to the formation of a strong force of British airborne troops, and the subsequent formation of The Glider Pilot Regiment. The recognition of the glider's potential to carry both troops and armaments directly to enemy positions was to play a key role in many important military confrontations in the years which followed the formation of this unique regiment.

The Glider Pilot Regiment was unique in two principal ways. First, it was a creature of the Second World War. Formed to fulfil a particular role in relation to that conflict and disbanded once that role had been fulfilled, it had perhaps the shortest active life of any regiment in British military history. Secondly, it combined in its pilots both the comprehensive skill of flying – all glider pilots were trained initially in the flying of powered aircraft – and of ground combat.

To this end Colonel George Chatterton, who commanded The Glider Pilot Regiment, secured the secondment of two Brigade of Guards warrant officers, both to instil discipline and to train the pilots to become 'total soldiers': pilots, who after landing their gliders behind enemy lines, were to become highly skilled fighting men.

In basing this book on the memories of many of the pilots who flew, without parachutes, in unpowered and defenceless aircraft, John Hemmings, himself a wartime glider pilot, brings to life many stories of gallantry, both in the air and on the ground, and celebrates the fortitude and dedication of the glider crews who, in the short life of the regiment, played such a crucial role in many of the great battles of Word War Two.

INTRODUCTION

Freight-carrying gliders pioneered in Britain

The combination of a powered aircraft towing a freight-carrying glider was first developed in Britain and is credited to best-selling author Barbara Cartland, who, with two former RAF officers, Messs Wenliss and Mole, carried out many tests during the 1920s before successfully carrying Royal Mail from Manston, Kent, to Reading, Berkshire, in the early 1930s. The mail-carrying continued for some time, until the Air Ministry banned it because of possible accidents in the air with other aircraft.

The Germans, never slow to recognise possibilities, seized on the idea of glider-towed combinations, and Hermann Goering, Adolf Hitler's head of the German Air Force – the Luftwaffe – saw the advantage of gliders in war, and so formed an army glider force which was built up to a peak of efficiency ready to be used if war came.

1

A Silent Approach

A German glider-borne assault on a Belgian fort

In the early morning darkness of 10 May 1940, ten German DFS gliders, towed by JU52 planes and carrying military demolition engineers and explosives, took off from Cologne to attack a Belgian fort sited at the confluence of the River Meuse and the Albert Canal, near Liège. Fort Emael was constructed of steel and concrete and was thought to be impregnable. It had heavily armoured turrets with 120 mm and 75 mm guns; anti-aircraft guns were sited within the massive structure, and the approaches were covered by anti-tank guns and machine-guns. In addition, a strong force of soldiers was stationed in the fort.

German reconnaissance planes had earlier taken photographs and while studying them Hitler saw that within the fort's perimeter walls was a large, flat, grassed area. He realised that gliders, making a silent approach and landing in the dark, would probably be unobserved. He reasoned that if the fort was captured, and the bridges over the Meuse and the Albert Canal were taken, a route would be opened for the rapid advance of Nazi troops and panzer divisions.

That is exactly what happened. A silent and undetected approach and landings by the gliders, before dawn, went unchallenged. The sound of the tug planes' engines was dismissed by the sentries as being just another air raid further away, a not unusual event. The sentries were overpowered, the garrison inside the Fort were unaware, and the German gliders landed directly onto the area of grass inside the fort's perimeter walls. The engineers, using hollow-explosive charges, quickly destroyed the gun emplacements, and the Belgian soldiers, many of them still asleep, were killed or taken prisoner, and the Germans went on to capture the bridges, and hold them, with only minimal casualties. The assault on Fort Emael and the bridges had been a complete success, a brilliantly executed *coup de main*.

2

An Elite Regiment

The Glider Pilot Regiment: how it was formed

When Winston Churchill, Britain's Prime Minister, received news of the raid from Allied intelligence, he recognised the value of a glider-borne military force and, determined that Britain would have one, he lost no time instructing his commanders to organise a glider regiment. There was, at first, considerable opposition, but Churchill insisted, and sent instructions to the War Office and the Combined Chiefs of Staff to raise an airborne force of glider pilots and paratroops by spring 1941. He also demanded confirmation that it was being done. His instruction was dated 23 June 1940, the day that France surrendered to Germany.

Winston Churchill was a determined man and a visionary. Throughout the war his charisma resulted in the British public pulling out all the stops to achieve results. It was Churchill's bulldog manner that led to the formation of The Glider Pilot Regiment and also the Parachute Regiment.

An establishment called the Central Landing School was set up at Ringway, near Manchester, for the study of the technicalities of gliders carrying troops, armaments and vehicles behind enemy lines. It also studied the technical details of parachuting. An officer from the Royal Engineers, Major John Rock, was appointed to command the army element but he was given no guidance. Neither did he have any flying experience or knowledge of parachuting. A staff officer, he also lacked experience of military training. To his credit, he was enthusiastic and soon called for volunteers from all army units, asking particularly for men with pre-war flying experience. Meanwhile, the army and the Royal Air Force began to work together. The RAF were to take charge of all flying training and both the War Office and the Air Ministry initiated designs for troop-carrying gliders, and eventually some prototypes were ordered from the General Aircraft Company Limited and Airspeed Limited.

A Glider Training Squadron was formed and it was joined by Lawrence Wright, an architect, who had formerly flown with the Royal Air Force; Timothy Hervey, who had flown during the First World War; and Robert Kronfield, a German Jew who had escaped from Nazi persecution, and who was an aeronautical expert. Then the first volunteers for glider pilot training began to arrive, among them Sergeant Malcolm Strathdee, who had earlier flown with the Royal Air Force. Bomber Command was growing rapidly, which led to the Air Ministry telling Winston Churchill that availability of planes for towing gliders and transporting parachutists was therefore restricted. The Prime Minister countered by demanding that he be informed of the progress of glider manufacture and the numbers of men who had volunteered for airborne service.

The Central Landing School was renamed the Central Landing Establishment, and it was quietly getting on with its job. The War Office estimated that the initial requirement of glider pilots would be 400, a number that would increase in course of time, depending upon how soon gliders became available and the RAF having both aircraft and instructors available. It was laid down, too, that all trainee glider pilots would undergo both powered aircraft and glider pilot training. Major Rock was busily liaising with the RAF and establishing a rapport.

The trainee glider pilots began by learning to fly powered planes, before going on to learn to pilot gliders, which were arriving from the factories.

Meanwhile, more gliders were becoming available and the trainee pilots were also receiving ground instruction similar to that being given to RAF pupil pilots. The selection of volunteers too was conducted on the lines of those for RAF aircrew volunteers, written and oral examinations and stringent medicals, all of which were conducted by Royal Air Force personnel

The first type of glider to become available was the Hotspur, a two-seater with the pilots sitting one behind the other. It was a lovely-looking machine, with graceful lines, and it proved to be an excellent training glider, capable of withstanding countless take-offs and landings under training conditions; those who flew them thoroughly enjoyed the experience.

Then came a larger glider, the Horsa, in which the two pilots sat side by side. It became the operational glider, carrying troops and equipment or alternatively, armaments and vehicles. It had a wingspan of 89 feet and a length of 68 feet, with a large perspex-covered cockpit, not unlike a small conservatory. It weighed 3.5 tons and could carry a load of the same weight. The tow rope, initially of hemp but later nylon, was fitted with a Y-shaped attachment that connected to the glider's wings at the leading edges, and the other end was fitted to the towing plane's tail. Both glider and plane were fitted with tow rope releases so that, after the glider had released, the tug plane could jettison the rope. Communication between both aircraft was by telephone, the line being woven into the tow rope, which, if overstretched, sometimes broke.

Late in 1940 the Glider Training Squadron moved south to Oxfordshire, and in the following spring Winston Churchill was an interested spectator of some demonstration flying. He later commented that the large Horsas, as large as the bombers towing them, required equal flying skills. Some RAF officer-pilots had been converted to flying gliders but the experiment did not last long as there was no shortage of army volunteers of all ranks.

On 21 December 1941, the Army Council approved the formation of The Glider Pilot Regiment and laid down that more than 600 men of all ranks, were to be trained for combat flying within 12 months. Major Rock was promoted to lieutenant colonel and given command of the new regiment. It was further laid down that the Royal Air Force would be responsible for the flying training of glider pilots. Brigadier Frederick 'Boy' Browning, Brigade of Guards, was appointed Officer Commanding the British 1st Airborne Division, of which The Glider Pilot Regiment was a part. A brilliant regular soldier, slim, dark and always immaculately dressed, he was respected by all who came into contact with him. He possessed an easy manner and would never ask anyone to do what he could not do himself. So, at the age of 46, he learned to fly and went solo in eight hours, the average for young pilots of less than half his age. John Rock too, learned to fly.

3

Brigadier George J.S. Chatterton

George Chatterton, a man of drive, personality, determination and enthusiasm, was, like Browning, always immaculately dressed. As a boy he was a cadet at Pangbourne Nautical College but, in 1930, he joined the Royal Air Force and became a commissioned pilot. While stationed at Tangmere, in West Sussex, he was one day flying a fighter plane in thick cloud, at 25,000 feet, when his aircraft was in collision with another. Although he used his parachute, it collapsed as he was nearing the ground and he sustained injuries that kept him in hospital for many months. When he eventually returned for active service he was told that he could no longer fly and was offered an administrative post. Unable to accept the situation, he resigned from the RAF, and subsequently joined a Territorial Army battalion, the Queen's Royal Regiment, as a lieutenant.

On the outbreak of war, called for active service, he went to France, where he was attached to a battalion of the Grenadier Guards. After Dunkirk, back in England, he volunteered to join The Glider Pilot Regiment and was appointed by 'Boy' Browning to be second in command to Lieutenant Colonel Rock.

The two men were complete opposites; Rock, a former staff officer, was quiet and more administratively orientated, whereas Chatterton was keen, forceful and outgoing, with an active-service background, both as an airman and a fighting soldier, and the two men did not always see eye-to-eye. Rock was not particularly strong on discipline; Chatterton, on the other hand, was appalled by the casual turnout of the pilots and trainee pilots and determined to smarten up everyone and everything. He realised that if the glider pilots were also to be combatant soldiers they needed discipline, footdrill, combat training and experience of handling all weapons. They also needed to be both highly skilled pilots and efficient, resourceful soldiers, and he immediately set to work to achieve that end. He went over the head of Rock and, with the help of Browning, brought two sergeant majors of the Brigade of Guards into the regiment and charged them with the task of making the pilots into what he termed *total soldiers*.

His men, he told the sergeant majors, were to have instilled into them a new personal pride and smartness of dress and he was determined that they would smarten themselves up, both sartorially and in a military sense. Foot drill and weapons drill were introduced, with the pilots learning to handle all types of weapons. Perhaps his main wish was that everyone in the regiment learned the immense value of *esprit de corps.*

While having those aims, Chatterton was experienced enough to weigh up the pros and cons of being a glider pilot and to consider not only the training required to prepare flying men for combat duties on the ground, but to recognise the problems involved. He recognised that piloting a glider on tow, releasing, and gliding down to land in hostile territory imposed a particular form of strain on the pilot, one that would not be alleviated by knowing that, after landing behind enemy lines, he would have no immediate prospect of returning whence he came. After flying for long distances, perhaps in difficult conditions, and having had the responsibility for the lives of the troops he had transported, he would be expected to use his flying skill and display determination and courage, to land on target, with the knowledge that he would immediately have to change identities and become a trained and resourceful soldier on the ground.

The Guards' sergeant majors, faced with training men in a newly formed regiment with no history and no tradition, set standards that the pilots responded to. The men of the RAF made fun of the 'Brown jobs', as the khaki-clad glider pilots were called, but the men responded to the challenge and, although a few fell by the wayside, unable to take it, the majority gave their full support to Chatterton and earned the reputation of being both highly skilled pilots and total soldiers.

Major Chatterton, as he then was, began to learn to fly gliders himself and quickly went solo in a Hotspur, having got through the stiff medical test despite the fact that, a few years earlier, he had been grounded following his flying accident while with the Royal Air Force. Meanwhile Lieutenant Colonel Rock was himself doing a glider course following upon his completion of training with Tiger Moths. During his absence George Chatterton had a free hand with the regiment, and at that time Captain Alistair Cooper, who had been at Pangbourne Nautical College at the same time as George Chatterton, joined The Glider Pilot Regiment. After leaving the college he had opted for the army and had served with the Cheshire Regiment as a regular officer and was soon to become Chatterton's Adjutant.

Then came a tragic accident that transformed the regiment. John Rock had qualified as a glider pilot, and one night he took up a Horsa loaded with sandbags to simulate a full load of soldiers. During the flight his tow rope broke and Rock was left in free flight and forced to make a landing in the dark, on unfamiliar ground. He got the Horsa down but then hit an unseen obstacle. The glider came to a sudden stop and the load of sandbags burst through the bulkhead, killing him instantly. His untimely death led to Major Chatterton taking command of the regiment and he was promoted to lieutenant colonel in October 1942.

Recalling a meeting in London with Lieutenant Colonel Chatterton, Captain Ron Dufton, Royal Artillery, said, 'While George and I were talking I felt that he was also assessing me as an officer, and I recall wondering whether my uniform, shoes and Sam Browne met with his approval. When I expressed interest in The Glider Pilot Regiment, he told me all of his pilots had to put in maximum effort, all of the time. They had, he said, to be able to endure pain and to be good leaders, whether they were officers, or NCOs. He always demanded absolute loyalty, both to himself and to the regiment.'

In 1943 Chatterton was promoted to full colonel, and assumed the title Commander, Glider Pilots. He piloted gliders in operations and his personality and enthusiasm reflected in his men; together they took The Glider Pilot Regiment to its unique place in military history. His glider pilots did all that was ever asked of them, reaching the highest levels of airmanship and gaining an unsurpassed reputation as combatants on the ground.

In 1945 George Chatterton, always 'George' to his pilots, received the honorary rank of brigadier.

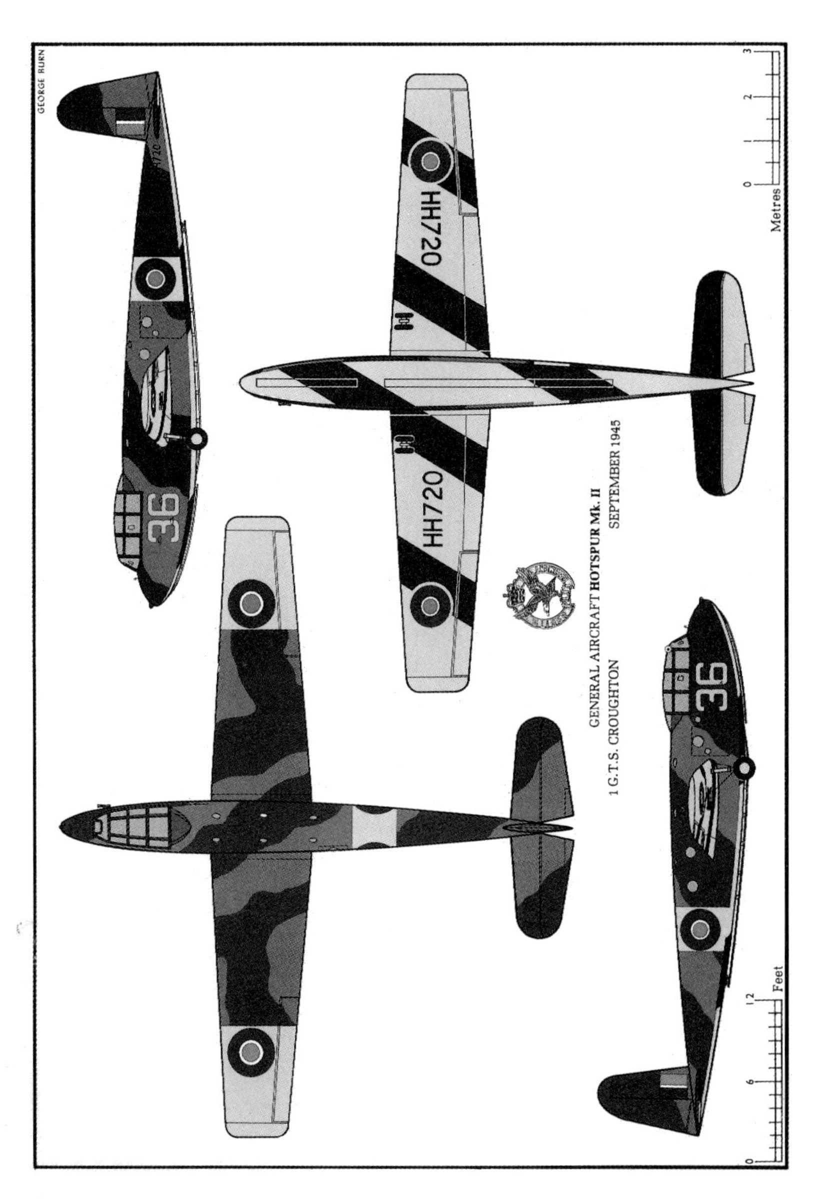

Hotspur training glider. 2 pilots sat one behind the other. Drawn by George Burn.

4

Norway 1943

Operation Freshman

During 1942 Allied intelligence learned that a heavy-water plant at Vermok, southern Norway, was to have its output stepped up. The plant was run by the occupying Germans, using forced labour, and heavy water (deuterium oxide) is a vital element of atomic bomb construction. The British decided therefore that the Vermok plant was to be used to construct atomic bombs and should be destroyed. The plant was located in a deep valley between mountains and presented problems of accessibility. Ways and means of attacking it were discussed in London. A bombing raid was discounted because of danger to homes in the vicinity. An assault by paratroops was discussed and abandoned because it was thought to be likely that a parachute drop would lead to the men being scattered over a wide area, and therefore open to detection. Likewise an attack by commandos from the sea was not considered to be practical. Thus the choice fell on The Glider Pilot Regiment, and two gliders were detailed for the assault.

The glider's passengers were men of the Royal Engineers who were explosives experts. The plan was for the two gliders to fly independently to Norway and to land at Mosvatnet, a five-hour trek over snow and rocks from the plant. They would be met by Norwegian agents, some of whom would guide them to the plant and others destroy all traces of the gliders. Near the plant the glider-borne party would be met by other Nowegians, who would guide them to the objective and after the raid assist them to escape, the escape route being a 200-mile journey over snow and mountains, on foot, travelling in twos and threes, to Sweden. They would not carry any means of identification and would travel in civilian clothes, worn under their uniforms.

Special Operations Executive (SOE) were asked to place the Norwegian agents at Mosvatnet and at Vermok. Having in mind the 500-mile tow to Norway, the long trek from Mosvatnet to Vermok and the even longer escape route, the Chief of SOE believed the plan to be ill-conceived, but was overruled.

Four pilots were selected from an original eight, the most experienced among them being Malcolm Strathdee, an early volunteer to the regiment. Each of the two gliders carried 15 Royal Engineers and their explosives. The planes chosen to tow them were Halifaxes, but because they were being used for bombing raids, they were not available until October 1942, after which the pilots and their crews had to undergo extensive training in towing loaded Horsas.

The other pilots selected for the operation were Sergeant Doig and two RAF pilots-cum-glider pilots, Pilot Officer Davies and Sergeant Fraser. They did some night flying, together with jettisoning their undercarriages and tail-down landings, as precautions for landing on snow-covered terrain. They also practised using a parachute attached to the tail of a Horsa, to be released on landing, to assist as a brake. Parachutes were not a standard attachment but it had been agreed that, for 'Freshman', a sudden landing in the snow, at speed, could be dangerous, with the Horsa being pulled up and burying its nose in the snow and perhaps turning turtle. The training included details of the landing zone operation by the Norwegian agents, and their escape route. They also studied a model of the plant that had been made from details supplied by agents. Assisted by the model, the pilots and Royal Engineers learned the positions of every window and door, the height of hedges and wire fencing, the movement of patrolling sentries, how long their beat lasted, where they passed and the frequency of their changes. The model details also gave the positions of machinery in the plant. All involved also underwent rigorous on-the-ground training, including long marches carrying heavy equipment, at night.

To assist the landing of the Horsas at the landing zone, a system of air-to-ground radio-beacon navigation aids, called Rebecca-Eureka, was devised. Rebecca was installed in each tug plane and Eureka was parachuted, before the operations, to the Norwegian agents on the ground. In operation, signals between ground and tug planes would enable the two Halifaxes to pinpoint the landing zone. Like the gliders, Eureka would be destroyed after landings had been made.

Shortly before the night of 19 November the four glider pilots and thirty sappers travelled to Skitten, north-east Scotland, from where the operation would begin. Take-off had been planned in daylight, but for technical reasons it was eventually delayed until after dark, and a forecast full moon failed to materialise. At the time of departure the weather was, in fact, quite poor. when Squadron Leader 'Wilkie' Wilkinson, one of the Halifax pilots, took up the towline slack, Sergeant Strathdee released his Horsa's wheelbrakes and the combination gathered speed; then the glider left the ground, the Halifax became airborne and the combination climbed through rain into cloud. A few minutes later the second Halifax and Horsa took off. Visibility was poor and ahead of the aircraft lay the long flight across the North Sea.

Six hours later, Skitten control tower received a signal from 'Wilkie' Wilkinson that he was returning to base.

After Wilkinson arrived back at Skitten and had landed his Halifax, he reported that the forecast moon and clear skies had not materialised. Cloud had thickened, but by using occasional gaps the squadron leader had reached the Norwegian coast at 10,000 feet, and had found the landing area. Unfortunately, however, Rebecca-Eureka had failed and they were unable to contact the Norwegian agents on the ground, neither could they see them in the darkness. The waiting agents had obviously thought it too risky to light landing flares, so Wilkinson, his Halifax fuel at the point of no return, decided that the combination should abort the landing and return to base in Scotland. Then, in cloud, the tow rope iced up and Wilkinson decided to lose height to reach a higher outside temperature and thaw the iced-up tow rope. But after flying a 100 miles or so, at 3,000 feet, the towline broke and Strathdee's Horsa was in free flight. The squadron leader, in his report, said that he believed that the combination had cleared the Norwegian coast and that the Horsa therefore must have gone down into the sea.

In fact the glider was still over land when the towline parted and the Horsa began to sink through thick cloud and falling snow. Malcolm Strathdee and Peter Doig strained their eyes searching for somewhere to land, but everything was blanketed out. Below them, unseen, was Hardanger Fjord, with the town of Stavanger at one end and a towering glacial mountain on one side.

Eventually the Horsa crashed, killing the two pilots and eleven of the sappers. The surviving four, injured, were later found by the Germans and taken to a prison hospital at Stavanger, where a German doctor tried to kill them by injecting air into their veins. The four men though, survived in great agony and were then strangled and their bodies thrown into the icy waters of the fjord.

The second Horsa had crossed the North Sea at a lower altitude to keep below the cloud base, and without seeeing anything of the other combination. Towed by its Halifax, it crossed the Norwegian coast and the tug pilot then turned south, towards Mosvatnet and the landing zone; but before they reached it the Halifax flew into a mountainside killing all of the crew. Most of those in the Horsa survived and were found by Norwegians, who attempted to get them to safety. Unfortunately they were unable to do so and they fell into German hands. The prisoners were taken to a barracks near Helleland, where, on the orders of the Gestapo commander, they were quickly executed.

Towards the end of the war, when British airborne troops arrived in Norway, the stories of the actrocities were told by Norwegians. The bodies of those killed in the first crash were exhumed from a common grave and reburied, with full military honours at Eiganes. Those whose bodies were thrown into the fjord are commemorated with a tablet. The writer has been to the pretty cemetery and has seen how carefully the local Norwegians and the War Graves Commission keep the headstones, which have flowers regularly placed by them. The bodies of those who died at Helleland were also reinterred with full military honours in the churchyard where their graves are carefully tended.

In October 1945, at a War Crimes Tribunal held in Oslo, the prison doctor and two others were found guilty of the murders at the prison hospital at Stavanger in 1942. Two were sentenced to death and the third received a life sentence. At another trial, the German Gestapo commander at Helleland was sentenced to death.

A Horsa Mk. 1 awaits towing out to the flight path.

With hindsight, Operation Freshman, as Sir Colin Gubbins, Head of SOE had believed, may have been ill-conceived and one cannot help but think that the glider pilots and their Royal Engineer passengers could not have rated their chances of success very high. If the two gliders had landed safely as planned, the occupants would have been faced with the ardous five-hour trek, carrying heavy equipment, over rocky snow-covered country to reach their objective. Then, if their mission at the plant had been successful, they were faced with the long 200-mile trek over mountains and through snow, in German-occupied territory, to reach the safety of Sweden. Would they have made it?

Not long afterwards Norwegian Underground members succeeded in causing damage at the heavy-water plant, forcing the Germans to move vital machinery to another area. While the parts were in transit and being ferried across a fjord, the boat carrying the parts was blown out of the water by charges pre-set by Norwegian patriots, and the vital pieces of machinery were lost for ever.

5

North Africa 1943

Operation-Turkey Buzzard

Early in 1943 a Joint Allied Planning Staff decided that Sicily should be the area of a big invasion by both airborne and seaborne forces. The capture of Sicily would open up the Mediterranean to Allied shipping, and also cause Italy a very serious blow that would reduce her to becoming a far weaker ally of Germany.

The plan was for gliders carrying infantry, weapons, jeeps trailers and ammunition, and elements of the Royal Artillery with guns and ammunition and vehicles, to land in advance of the seaborne troops and to capture and hold key bridges and other points. The Glider Pilot Regiment was ordered to send two squadrons, by sea, from England to North Africa, where they would collect gliders shipped out. The remainder of the regiment's pilots would move to the south west of England with their gliders, ready to move to North Africa when called.

Colonel Chatterton and the men of the two squadrons sailed to Oran on 13 April 1943, from where they travelled 60 miles overland to Tizi, on the Mascara Plain, where they were billeted in tents. Later, 50 pilots were sent back to Oran to collect American Waco Gliders that had been shipped from the United States. On arrival, however, the glider pilots found the Wacos in pieces, still packed in the crates in which they had been shipped. So, with the aid of handbooks, the pilots began to assemble the parts into finished gliders. They had not been provided with any quarters, so as the wooden crates were emptied they took them over as sleeping accommodation. The gliders, when assembled were then transported to an airstrip and later towed by American Dakotas to Tizi.

Colonel Chatterton decided to take a Waco into the air himself, as they were unfamiliar to him. The Waco was smaller than the Horsa and its nose lifted to allow men and cargo to enter and exit from the front. He was agreeably surprised with the experience and in particular the way the Waco handled.

The pilots waiting in England were eventually briefed for the 1,500 mile flight to Tunisia. Three pilots were allotted to each glider to provide relief during the long haul. Whilst waiting for the order to join their fellow pilots in North Africa they had undergone three months of intensive preparation, during which time one Halifax–Horsa combination had flown 1,500 miles around Britain, to prove that a tow of that length could be done.

The route from Portreath to Tunisia would take them over the Bay of Biscay, to avoid flying over Europe, and it was known that German JU88s and Focke-Wulf Condors were active in that area.

Captain Eric Kettle said, 'Many glider pilots and tug crews experienced misgivings because it was known that German planes had scored a number of successes, shooting down Allied planes over the Bay of Biscay, and tug planes and glider combinations were not too manoeuverable when coming under attack. The glider pilots realised that they would probably have to release to give the tug plane's gunners a clear field of fire, and that they, the glider pilots, would have to take their chances in the sea; and it was not then known whether a Horsa or Hamilcar would float!'

A Horsa crewed by Major A.J. Cooper and Sergeant's Sotiris Antonopoulos and D. Hall began the long journey to North Africa and with Cooper at the controls arrrived over the Bay of Biscay.

The combination flew into cloud, and being unable to see the tug plane, the glider got out of position and the tow rope broke. While the pilot concentrated on the descent the other two went aft to collect a dinghy, an axe with which to cut their way out of the glider, some water and emergency rations. The Horsa made a perfect landing but immediately began to fill with water. Breaking out, the three pilots climbed onto a wing, inflated the dinghy and their life jackets, left the Horsa and drifted away. For many hours they saw no shipping, but during the night a Royal Navy frigate found them and returned them to the UK, landing them in Northern Ireland, from where they were returned to Portreath.

Twenty-four hours later Antonopoulos and Hall were in the air again, the third pilot that time being Staff Sergeant Conway, en route for Sale, Tunisia. Fate again took a hand as they crossed the Bay of Biscay. This time two Focke Wulf Condors attacked the combination. The Halifax gunners opened fire and the tug captain asked Antonopoulos, who was at the controls of the Horsa, to release. Reluctantly he called to Hall to do so, and while the Halifax's guns were blazing the Horsa lost height and Antonopoulos made a good landing on the sea. The pilots collected a dinghy, flares, emergency rations and an axe, then broke their way out and got onto a wing, where they inflated the dinghy and their life jackets.

They calculated that, at the speed the dinghy was drifting, it would probably be several days before they reached neutral but friendly Portugal.

They saw a Halifax–Horsa combination pass overhead and sent up a flare. The weather worsened and the waves got bigger. The next day they sighted a ship as they went up onto the crest of a wave and fired another flare, but again failed to be seen. The circular-shaped dinghy made little headway and it began to ship water, despite continuous baling-out by the three pilots. Their feet were constantly in water and their hands blistered. As the days passed they carefully rationed their water, kept baling and slipped in and out of delirium.

On the tenth day it became very sunny and hot, causing the pilots more discomfort, then the eleventh day was very misty and they were near exhaustion, but a Spanish fishing boat appeared beside them and they were taken aboard and landed at Vigo, Spain, although neutral, had a sympathy towards Germany, so the pilots were taken into custody by the police until rescued by the British Vice-Consul. They were suffering from exposure, malnutrition and dehydration, plus the effects of having had their feet continually in sea water, but after a few days spent recovering, they were taken south to Gibraltar, from where they were returned to England.

They did eventually get to Tunisia and they, and Major Alistair Cooper, all took part in the Sicily invasion, where Alistair Cooper lost his life.

Jimmy Pearce, a perky cockney sergeant who worked on a national newspaper before the war, jettisoned the Horsa's undercarriage as they left Portreath. That was a normal practice under certain conditions, to reduce drag and save fuel for the tug plane's long haul. Extra fuel tanks had been fitted in the bomb bays of each Halifax to give additional range, but any drag caused by the wheels of gliders could result in fuel wastage. They were lucky not to be intercepted, and reached Tunisia safely. Jimmy went on to take part in the Sicily assault, was wounded and lost an eye, but eventually returned to his beloved Fleet Street, where he worked until his death in 1978.

Nigel Brown was at the controls of a Horsa that flew out of Portreath and he and his two co-pilots spent ten hours behind their tug, many of them at a low altitude. Their undercarriage too had been jettisoned and they landed at Sale on the Horsa's skids. The journey had not been without its problems; the clouds were down to sea level and at one stage Brown could not see the Halifax towing them. When they did emerge into clearer weather he still could not see the Halifax, but his co-pilots saw the plane –

it was below them, the Horsa was almost on top of it!

Another Horsa crossed the Moroccan coast and was soon over Sale. The pilot put the glider down smoothly and it slid to a perfect stop on its skids, to the cheers of servicemen and Arabs.

Staff Sergeant Gordon Jenks accidentally jettisoned his glider's undercarriage while still over the runway at Portreath, and one oleo leg bounced up and became stuck in the glider's wing. There was a hurried telephone talk between Jenks and the tug pilot, then they decided to carry on and they completed the journey without further incident.

The Halifaxes towing gliders out had to refuel and then return to England, to repeat the tow with another glider. One of them caught fire almost immediately after leaving Morocco and crashed, killing the crew. Another which failed to return to Cornwall was presumably shot down.

Bill Chambers, Ron Owen and another pilot reached Sale after the long haul from Cornwall, arriving tired but pleased to have achieved 1,500 miles of flying successfully. Their euphoria evaporated though, when, after a rest, they were detailed to fly with other Horsas to Algeria, to join American Wacos already there. Having done so, they were all moved to the Tunisian airstrips from which the attack on Sicily would be made. It meant flying across the high spine of North Africa, where turbulence above the peaks caused some dramatic losses of height in stomach-heaving circumstances. The sun was extremely hot, the Horsas' cockpits became very uncomfortable, and the tug planes' engines heated up.

Richard Martin was one of the glider pilots in camp at Sousse when a nearby ammunition dump caught fire and then blew up in a series of spectacular but alarming 'fireworks' in multicolours. The heat was intense and everyone evacuated the burning scrub, with pieces of red-hot metal flying around. Amazingly there were no serious injuries.

The tug plane thunders down the runway and the Horsa is airborne.

As the date for the assault on Sicily drew nearer, with aircrews and glider-borne troops getting to know each other, living in tents with the wastelands around them, the men thought often of their first operation and the airlift they were to be a part of, the biggest airborne assault ever carried out by any nation.

Colonel Chatterton's thoughts too were on the coming airborne lift and he worried that many of his pilots had not made long night flights of the type they would undertake to fly from North Africa to Sicily. Aerial photographs taken of the proposed landing zones in Sicily also bothered him. The photographs revealed that they were rock-strewn and had small fields, with a predominance of stone walls, and a lot of wooded areas He knew that landings in the dark would not be easy. The Italian army were deployed defending the coast, and German mobile troops were in reserve further back. Worse, the glider pilots had little experience of night flying.

The first night of the operation would be a glider operation, with no parachutists involved, and the glider-borne troops were to capture the bridges near Syracuse and also the town itself. Paratroops would be dropped on the following night, with the task of capturing the port of Augusta, and a third attack would be by paratroops and gliders carrying guns and vehicles, around the Primasole Bridge and Catania Plain, their task to hold their objectives until the British 8th Army met them.

Colonel Chatterton's brief to his glider pilots was that they would land by moonlight, after releasing from their tugs at 2,000 feet. The glider loads would be infantry, jeeps and artillery. For the third attack, the Horsas would carry six-pounder guns and jeeps in support of the 1st Parachute Brigade. There would be seven Horsas and eight Wacos, towed by Halifaxes and Albemarles. In the weeks before the invasion date the weather was hot and the air still, but during the 48 hours before the operation the wind began to blow until it reached gale force and this state continued until the day of take-off, when gliders on the six airstrips to be used were ready and waiting.

6

Sicily, 9–12 July 1943

Operation Ladbroke

At 1400 hours, when the signal came for take-off, Colonel Chatterton, at the controls of the lead glider, heard the Dakota tug plane start up and the tow rope tautened. Dust and grit swirled, the combination moved forward and they were airborne. Chatterton's adjutant, Captain Harding, was his co-pilot and the passengers were Brigadier Hicks, his Brigade Chief Medical Officer and staff officers. Flying conditions were not good and Chatterton, due to reach the landing zone at 2200 hours, did not relish the thought of an eight-hour flight.

Lieutenant 'Woody' Birch, piloting a Waco, wondered whether the glider force might be attacked by enemy fighter planes. He recalls the strong wind and the air turbulence and also that the leader of the platoon of the South Staffordshire Regiment he was carrying being airsick. 'Woody' and his co-pilot, Sergeant Wright, were bathed in perspiration as they struggled to keep the glider flying straight and level at just 200 feet to avoid radar, only gaining height as they approached the release point. Then enemy guns began firing and tracer began to appear all around them. A searchlight picked them up just as they released and Birch found himself busily engaged as they descended, at the same time trying to lose the searchlight. Twice shells, or pieces of shrapnel, hit the glider's wings, but the Waco kept flying. Most of his flying had been in Horsas but Birch liked the way in which the Waco approached its landing in a longer shallow glide, as opposed to the Horsa's steeper angle, as the glide took the glider further in when he reached the landing area. They came under fire on the ground and took temporary cover, but a lance corporal in the glider opened fire with his sten gun and the enemy, numbers unknown, retreated long enough for Lieutenant Birch and the others to move off in the direction of their objective, the Ponte Grande which spanned a highway and two canals, having a few short exchanges of fire on the way.

Staff Sergeant Galpin released, but found himself over Syracuse itself, north of the Ponte Grande that spanned two canals. He turned his glider on a course set by his co-pilot and soon afterwards saw the landing zone. Almost immediately a searchlight locked onto the glider, followed by salvo after salvo of ack-ack shells. Galpin's evasive action took the glider out to sea but he lost height and turned back towards the landing zone, the searchlight following. Fortunately it illuminated both the field in which he was to land and the bridge. He landed safely, but while the glider was running forward its nose wheels went into a deep depression in the ground, the wheels broke and the underside of the nose was damaged.

The platoon quickly disembarked and they all raced to the bridge, which was quickly captured. Galpin and his co-pilot took some prisoners, and as first light came, an element of the 1st Air Landing Brigade joined them. There were also some other glider pilots at the bridge. During the morning Italian troops counter-attacked, supported by mortars. Casualties were heavy on both sides and, outnumbered and almost out of ammunition, the Italians eventually retreated.

Carrying the Commanding Officer of the Royal Artillery, his staff and a 6-pounder gun, Major Alistair Cooper was flying his glider through a barrage of tracer shells when the tug plane towing him was hit and exploded. Cooper's glider was at only 500 feet, a quarter of the pre-arranged release height, and still over the sea, when he found himself in free flight. The low altitude made it difficult for him to reach land but he just cleared a cliff-top before crashing, and everyone aboard was killed.

Staff Sergeant Nick English had been released by the Dakota towing him when it turned away from heavy flak. The glider was then too far from land to reach the landing zone and it went down on the sea. English, his co-pilot and a platoon of the Border Regiment swam ashore. On the way they saw other gliders in the sea and men swimming, not all of whom reached land. Nick and his party reached a beach between cliffs on one side and Syracuse on the other. Tired, wet and unarmed, they were taken prisoner by Italian troops and marched inland a few miles and then allowed to rest until daybreak. They were well treated and given food and drink before being marched off again to a temporary prisoner-of-war camp, from where they were later moved to a succession of prison camps in Germany.

In the intense darkness as they approached Sicily, Captain Ken Monroe recalls the sudden illumination by searchlights and tracer. Both Monroe and 'Nobby' Clarke, his co-pilot, were blinded by the searchlights and found it difficult to see, but by straining his eyes 'Nobby' eventually picked out features below memorised from aerial photographs. After release, with Clarke calling out height and speed, Monroe eventually levelled out and landed the Waco safely. The South Staffords aboard quickly unloaded everything and on a compass bearing, set off across country. Explosions and gunfire led them towards the objective and Monroe sent two infantrymen forward to recce. They returned to say that the Ponte Grande was the scene of fighting and that two glider pilots were there firing an anti-tank gun. Monroe and the others went forward to join the glider pilots and infantrymen already at the bridge.

Staff Sergeant Ken Evans piloted a glider carrying a platoon of the Border Regiment under the command of Sergeant Cherry. Their objective was the Ponte Grande. The wind was strong and the long flight unpleasant in the darkness, flying at only 200 feet to avoid radar. The telephone between glider and tug had failed and they had no communication. Approaching the Sicilian coast, the pilot of the Dakota towing them suddenly banked and turned to starboard, then began a steep climb, zigzagging as he did so to avoid anti-aircraft shellfire. The Dakota's manoeuvres put a great strain on the tow rope but it did not break. However, they had flown away from Sicily, out to sea, and had lost sight of the other glider–tug plane combinations.

When he released, Evans' glider was picked up by a searchlight, and tracer shells burst around them. He managed to get away from the searchlight but his vision had been affected by the strong light. As the glider descended, he saw a cliff looming up but managed to haul the glider over the top of it just missing some high-tension wires before hitting the top of a stone wall, which effectively brought the glider to a stop. In the crash, Evans' foot was broken and he also suffered a chest injury. Richard Martin, his co-pilot, suffered a green-stick fracture of the left femur and other injuries. Three of the Borderers were also injured. Sergeant Cherry had the five men lifted out of the glider and laid in the shade of the glider's wings, before taking the rest of his men to find their objective. Sometime later a roving medical orderly found the injured men and gave them first aid and he improvised splints. While he was attending to them, an enemy plane appeared and began to fire around the crashed glider. Without hesitation the medical orderly threw himself down and spreadeagled himself across the two glider pilots, shielding them. Fortunately no one was hit but it was a splendid example of selfless heroism, says Kenneth Evans.

The glider had landed well away from the main force because of the tug plane's manoeuvring, so there were no other British troops in the vicinity. However, Sergeant Cherry, who had gone off with his men, did report the location of the crashed glider and the injured men, and in course of time they were found and taken to a hospital in Syracuse that was staffed by nuns. From there they were later taken to a landing craft, where the five men lay on the deck in the blazing sun for several hours before being put aboard a hospital ship and taken to a hospital in Tunisia.

Fighting in the area of the Ponte Grande was hotting up, with the enemy using heavy machine-guns and from further away, mortars and a field gun were directed onto the attackers. The Italians outnumbered the Allied troops but they lacked courage, or they would have overrun the airborne men, who had suffered a number of casualties. A number of glider pilots were holding the bridge, among them Dick Foster, a lieutenant, who had piloted a Waco with his co-pilot Terry Brady. They, like so many others, had been released short of the pre-arranged release point but had safely made it to land, after which they had found their way to the bridge, together with the men of the South Staffordshire Regiment that they had flown from North Africa. They arrived just before the prisoners that Galpin and others had put into a blockhouse at the bridge were killed by a direct hit from an Italian field gun.

In his Waco, Colonel Chatterton was nearing his release point, feeling the strain of piloting the glider in difficult conditions for the whole journey. Captain Harding had been airsick continually and unable to give the colonel relief. The Dakota pilot wished them good luck as they released and headed towards land, about 2 miles distant. The searchlights snapped on and tracer began to burst. The Waco's starboard wing was hit and when it was down to only 200 feet the wing crumpled and the Waco fell towards the sea. Chatterton managed to pancake it, and after it hit the water the pilots, with Brigadier Hicks and his staff, clambered out and onto the sound wing. Almost immediately they came under attack from a machine-gun and prudently Chatterton and the others slid down into the water and began to swim. Unharmed, they reached a small beach and lay under the overhang of a cliff, watching gliders above illuminated by searchlights. They saw some go down into the sea and some tug planes too were hit. They later learned that many of the men were drowned, or killed in the air. Others, like the colonel and his party, got ashore.

At first light, Chatterton, the brigadier and others moved off the beach, after having been joined by a small group of Special Air Service (SAS) men who had landed from a naval pinnace. As they advanced up the cliff they had various skirmishes with the enemy and took some prisoners, whom they later handed over to some British troops. By that time the shelling had increased. On their journey Colonel Chatterton's group passed many gliders that had landed during the night, some undamaged but many wrecked and one burnt out. In one, a 6-pounder anti-tank gun had burst through the bulkhead, killing the pilots and those being carried. An explosion in another had blown all the occupants forward, leaving a tragic pile of bodies at the front. Chatterton, the brigadier and others eventually reached the bridge, where they met up with General Browning, 1st Airborne Division Commander, who had also reached Sicily in a glider. Together they drove into Syracuse.

Glider pilot 'Tug' Wilson landed safely, but soon after those aboard had unloaded and begun to make their way to join others, they were taken prisoner and marched towards Avola. However, en route Wilson seized his chance and dropped unseen into a ditch. When all was quiet he emerged and later met up with men of the Durham Light Infantry, with whom he stayed.

One glider, piloted by Captain Denholme, landed close to the Ponte Grande bridge. He had released and then flown almost 5 miles to the field he had to find in the dark, but landed downwind, very fast, and ran into the canal bank, causing a Bangalore torpedo being carried in the glider to explode. Denholme and all in the glider with him were thrown forward and killed.

At the bridge, Dennis Galpin and the others continued to hold out, despite casualties, and it was not until the afternoon of 10 July, after an action lasting around nine hours, during which their ammunition was expended, that the Italians re-took the bridge. Nearby was another small force, 16 glider pilots under the command of Lieutenant Boucher-Giles. They too held out until their ammunition was gone and were then taken prisoner. However, they did not remain prisoners long as a number of men of the Northamptonshire Regiment arrived, killed the Italians and freed the glider pilots.

Troops advance in Sicily.

On one of the Tunisian airstrips a Dakota revved up and a Waco glider rose into the air. The first pilot, Staff Sergeant Tom Moore, looked at the 2nd pilot, Sergeant Ivan Garrett, sitting beside him. It was Ivan's birthday and one that he was to remember until he died. Behind them were 12 infantrymen of the South Staffordshire Light Infantry, four handcarts of ammunition, an assortment of weapons and a Bangalore torpedo. Soon after taking off, the perspex panel in the cockpit blew out and the inrush of air caused discomfort to everyone, and also generated a lot of noise. Near to the point of release a searchlight caught them. The tug pilot dived in an attempt to lose it, and together Dakota and Waco went down almost to the sea. Climbing again, they reached 2,000 feet and Moore released and headed towards the shore.

The landing, on very rocky ground, broke the glider's wheels. It slid forward, fast, then hit an unseen rock and came to an abrupt stop. The glider's nose was smashed and the impact broke Moore's ankle and pinned his legs under his seat. Garrett was unhurt and broke his way out of the cockpit to try to help the men inside. The glider had landed near an Italian pillbox from which phosphorus grenades were thrown. One or two of them fell on top of the Waco and pieces of burning material fell through the roof and onto the top of the handcarts filled with ammunition. Some of the infantrymen had been killed and wounded in the crash and Garrett tried to pull some of the survivors out of the burning glider. The ammunition exploded and Garrett's left elbow was almost torn out. Undeterred, he went to the front of the Waco and with his one good arm lifted the nose a little, enough for Tommy Moore to drag his legs free, but the effort caused one of his legs to break. The two pilots took cover, while the surviving infantrymen, led by their corporal, attacked the pillbox, killing the Italian soldiers. However, during the attack a grenade burst close to the corporal, badly injuring both his knees. Moore tried to apply field dressings but the corporal's wounds were too big. He also bandaged Garrett's elbow but could see that the wound was serious and had rendered the arm useless. Later, Garrett's arm blackened; he had lost a lot of blood and lapsed in and out of unconsciousness. He was also suffering from the cold. As daylight came, Moore could see that the tourniquet he had applied was sodden with blood.

In the early morning light Moore could see the invasion fleet coming over the horizon, every conceivable type of ship, side by side. Then, as he watched, invasion barges began to head for the shore, towards a point a mile or two from where Tom Moore was. His spirits rose, believing that he and the others might be found. Between the burned out glider and the point at which the barges were landing was a strip of land held by the Italians, and their planes began to strafe the troops coming ashore at Avola. Knowing that Garrett and the corporal needed urgent medical attention, Moore decided to seek help. He dragged himself towards the beach and came across a dead Italian. He took a carbine from the corpse and used it to fashion an improvised splint and then made his painful way to the beach, crossing two wire fences on the way. At the water's edge he collapsed and came to with both his legs in the water. Revived, he decided to try to swim to one of the ships but had to give up and return to the beach. Then he decided to try to get along the beach to Avola. On the way he found a piece of driftwood; he made a splint from it and further on he took a length of wood from a fence to make himself a crutch.

Between him and Avola were some farm buildings, close to the beach, and he headed towards them. After lying for a while studying them, he decided that the farm had been deserted, so he went to the farmhouse and looked for food. As he was leaving he saw a figure coming along a path towards the farmhouse. It was propelling itself backwards, on its elbows and posterior. Then he saw it was the wounded corporal. They joined forces and were about to leave when they saw some Italian soldiers coming towards the farmhouse, pushing a mobile machine-gun. They hid and eventually the Italians continued on their way. When the coast was clear Tommy Moore and the corporal set off back towards the place where Ivan Garrett lay. Hearing voices, they froze, but were relieved when a medical officer, with a stretcher

A Horsa takes off.

party from an Indian division, appeared. The medical officer did what he could for the two men, sent for extra stretcher parties, and then went along the path to find Garrett, who by then was suffering from gangrene, loss of blood and exposure. Later the three men were carried to Avola and evacuated to Tripoli, where they remained for several months before being returned to hospitals in England.

Relating this story, Tommy Moore said that Ivan Garrett lost his arm and the corporal learned that he would never again bend his knees. 'Ivan Garrett undoubtedly saved my life when, though grievously wounded, he got me out of the burning glider. We remained close friends until his death from cancer.'

7

Day 3 – Sicily

Operation Fustian 11–12 July 1943

'Fustian' was planned to follow on after the main attack on Sicily, on Day 3. Its purpose was to attack and capture a second bridge, the Ponte Primosole, situated north of Syracuse and crossing the River Simento which flows through the Catania Plain. The operation was to be mainly by the British 21st Independent Parachute Company, followed in by ten Horsas and eight Wacos carrying anti-tank guns, ammunition and vehicles. The paratroops were carried by American Air Force Dakotas, and the gliders were towed by Halifaxes and Albemarles. Flying from North Africa, they followed the same course as their comrades had on Day 1. Their landing zones were around the bridge itself and a few miles north-west.

Their approach took them over the Allied invasion fleet with disastrous results. German aircraft had earlier bombed the vast fleet, and the gunners on the warships guarding them had been warned to expect another attack. When they heard the engines of the approaching para transports, followed by the tug planes and gliders, they went immediately into action and pounded the planes overhead unmercifully. The fact that a signal had been sent advising the approach of the transports, tugs and gliders, was overlooked. Frantic recognition signals from the aircraft were ignored and the heavy anti-aircraft fire inflicted serious losses, damage and casualties. Ten of the transport planes were blown out of the sky and four of the tugs towing gliders were shot down, their crews lost together with the gliders. One of the towing Halifaxes lost was piloted by Squadron Leader Wilkinson, who had survived the ill-fated Operation Freshman eight months earlier. Twenty-seven of the Dakotas carrying paratroops turned back and headed for North Africa in the confusion. So, before the survivors got onto the ground their numbers had been very seriously depleted.

Sergeant Roy Dudley was co-pilot to Staff Sergeant Wallis, who was at the controls as they flew behind their tug through the naval barrage. He said, 'Wallis was hit by a piece of shrapnel that made his shoulder a bit of a mess and I immediately took over the controls, the thought passing through my mind that if I were hit and couldn't fly the glider, it would crash. We were looking for the landing zone in the darkness, where the paras should have laid out a flare path but had not done so; however, it didn't seriously matter as Italian searchlights were giving off some reflected light that was helpful. Then we came under automatic fire and a bullet passed through the floor, between Dick Wallis and myself, and out through the top without doing any real damage. I made my approach to land and touched down too fast, but the uneven ground helped us to stop close to where we should have been, shaken but unhurt.

'While the anti-tank gun, ammunition and jeep were unloaded, I did what I could for Dick, applying a field dressing. I was going to leave him under cover, but he insisted on going with us to the bridge and later acted as a loader when one of the gunners was killed. At the bridge there were other glider pilots, among them Sergeant Atkinson, all of whom fought with distinction and the Ponte Primosole was seized and held until we were relieved.'

Among the gliders flying from North Africa was a Waco piloted by Richard Hanson and Jock East. As they neared the coast of Sicily they could see searchlights and flak from the enemy defences ahead of them and they were awaiting the signal from the tug plane to release the tow rope from the glider. Suddenly, without any warning, their tug plane released the tow rope from the plane so that it fell away, still attached to the Waco and hanging below the glider's nose. They were not near enough to reach land and as they prepared to ditch they saw the tug plane bank and swing away, setting course for North Africa.

Lieutenant Colonel John Place, who had become second in command to Colonel George Chatterton, was made responsible for the programme of training for the British glider pilots to fly the American Wacos. For the Sicily operation, Major General Hopkinson, commanding 1st Airborne Division, chose to fly in Place's glider. Following the Sicily operation, what remained of the 1st Battalion returned to North Africa, with 2 and 3 Squadrons continuing with a programme of training on Wacos. The general was subsequently killed in Italy.

B.P. 'Paddy' Feehily, together with Tony Plowman, flew a Horsa from North Africa for the Sicily operation, but, after seven hours' night flying, their glider went down into the sea and they were subsequently picked up and landed in Italy, returning to Algiers before the end of the year. Paddy went on to become regimental sergeant major at The Glider Pilot Regiment's Fargo depot, Larkhill. A regular soldier, he was commissioned after the war and attained the rank of lieutenant colonel.

These are but a few of the experiences of glider pilots given to the author by men whose memories remain clear, or who were helped by references to diaries and logbooks. Some were openly critical of the circumstances that led to many having to ditch in the sea, or having to release so far out that they were unable to reach the coast without difficulty. Many of them were decorated for their courage and skills.

Major General Montgomery praised the regiment; he believed the capture of the Ponte Grande in particular, had saved the 8th Army many days of fighting, which in turn reduced their casualties. General Hopkinson, who had flown with his troops to Sicily, was forthright in his condemnation of the American Dakota pilots. However, in his report General Alexander, always a fair man, said that the inexperience of the American Dakota pilots flying unarmed, slow aircraft was responsible for their inability to take all the gliders close in before they released. In his turn, Colonel Chatterton was unhappy with an operation that had been a nightmare, that had cost too many lives and the loss of too many aircraft. Indeed, the aftermath of the first-ever Allied Airborne invasion was very sensitive and on his return to Tunisia Colonel Chatterton was instructed to order his glider pilots not to enter into arguments with members of the American Air Force.

Perhaps it was that too much had been expected of everyone, the transport and tug plane pilots, the glider pilots and the infantry units involved. Both the British and Americans lacked experience of such an invasion, and the bad weather and poor visibility, combined with the hilly coast and rocky terrain, and a night landing, were all contributory factors to a very difficult invasion. Fifty-seven glider pilots were killed and many more wounded. Of those carried in gliders, more than 600 were killed, missing or wounded.

Those who saw fit to advise Colonel Chatterton to order his glider pilots not to tangle with the Americans need not have worried. Glider pilots, however disgruntled they may have been initially, were very resilient and very soon began to integrate and socialise with American aircrews.

A Horsa glider just airborne at the end of its towrope.

8

North Africa

Operation Elaborate, August – September 1943

Since the invasion of Sicily the number of RAF planes made available for towing gliders had not appreciably increased, but the situation subsequently improved. General Eisenhower asked for 25 Horsas to be sent to North Africa urgently, and the operation was code-named Elaborate. Halifaxes of 295 Squadron, RAF, were also chosen to go and the ferrying was carried out between 15 August and 23 September 1943, with the combinations again flying from Portreath, Cornwall, to Kairouan, with three pilots allotted to each glider.

As in the case of the earlier Operation Turkey-Buzzard, many of the journeys proved hazardous. One combination was attacked over the Bay of Biscay, by a number of German JU88 aircraft and the glider went down in the sea, but fortunately the three pilots were later picked up by a naval vessel after having been sighted by a passing aircraft. Eight other gliders had to cast off from their tug planes for various reasons, one only a few miles from the North Africa coast, and the three pilots were picked up by a passing friendly vessel. Two Horsas, cast off because of their tugs having engine problems, landed safely in neutral Portugal, from where they returned to Portreath, and one made a landing in Spain but eventually, after early difficulties, they returned to Portreath via Gibraltar.

On another occasion, a Horsa went down into the sea but the crew were picked up by an Air Sea Rescue boat. Unhappily the three pilots of another glider, who had to release from the tug plane when it was attacked, went down into the Bay of Biscay but were not rescued and were subsequently posted as missing, believed drowned.

It was later reported that all the glider pilots taking part in Operation Elaborate displayed courage and skill during the flights. Unfortunately, I was unable to make contact with any of the pilots who took part in the operation and have relied upon this information from two former glider pilots, Victor Wade and Ken Dexter.

For the Allies, their landing on Sicily was symbolic, because it meant that they were once again fighting on European soil

The campaign was short, but effective, and Italy was no longer to be considered as a serious ally of the Germans. Only two months after the landing on Sicily the Italians forced the head of its government, dictator Benito Mussolini, and his Fascist Cabinet to resign. The new government, led by Marshal Badoglio, then asked the Allies for an armistice, which was signed on 3 September. Germany, however, still had troops in strength on the Italian mainland.

9

Changes

Colonel Chatterton, at that time, adopted the title Commander, Glider Pilots, although there was no official establishment for such an appointment. His adjutant, Captain Peter Harding, was promoted to major and became Chatterton's staff officer at 38 Group, RAF Headquarters, with a junior officer and two sergeants to assist him.

During the Sicily campaign period the 6th Airborne Division had been formed. Actually it was the 2nd, but was called the 6th to mislead the Germans as to Britain's strength. Major General Richard Gale was appointed its commander and the intention was that it would operate as a single formation, rather than in brigades like 1st Airborne Division. Major General Sir Frederick Browning had been appointed Major General Airborne Forces.

Colonel Chatterton conceived the idea that the Royal Air Force and The Glider Pilot Regiment would work more closely together, with the crews of the towing planes – pilot, navigator, engineer and gunner – and the first and second glider pilots more integrated, as a team. Until then glider pilots, as army personnel, were not really close to the RAF pilots and crews. Chatterton's persistence led to closer team spirit, and also to the establishment of first and second pilots to assist the training programme. The second pilot's rank was sergeant, as opposed to the first pilot being a staff sergeant, or more senior. The second pilot would get his wings after some 30 hours' training, after which time he was examined as to his competence to take over the flying of a glider in an emergency and also to land it. There were many occasions when such action had to be taken, at which time the co-pilots proved to be most competent.

The second pilot was identified by the wings he wore; they were of a different design to those of the first pilot, and smaller. Another innovation at that time was that glider pilots were sent on maintenance courses.

A mention has to be made of the regiment's cap badge, worn on a maroon beret; it was ornamented with an eagle, wings outstretched, standing on the letters AAC, within laurel leaves surmounted by a crown. Unusually for a regimental badge, it was silver.

10

Twin-Hotspur

An unusual version of the Hotspur training glider was tested by the army. It was a unique form of transportation known as the GAL 48B and comprised two conventional Hotspurs fastened to

General Aircraft 'Twin' Hotspur. Drawn by George Burn.

each other side by side, with a common centre section and tailplane. Inevitably called the Twin-Hotspur, the only example had the serial number MP486/G – the G meaning that it required special guarding: secret list. It first flew in August 1942, towed by a Whitley V BD505. The pilot sat in the port fuselage with a full set of conventional controls, there being none in the starboard fuselage. The design doubled the carrying capacity of the glider, which could carry 16 armed soldiers. A noteworthy feature of the glider was the introduction of a wheel at each side of the landing skids under both booms.

Experimental flying came to an end when the Twin-Hotspur eventually crashed, leading to the project being abandoned.

'Twin Hotspur'.

11

Hamilcar Squadron

From the earliest days of The Glider Pilot Regiment a large glider capable of carrying light tanks, field guns, gun-hauling vehicles, trucks, bridge-building materials, as well as heavy ammunition and men, had been in various stages of design and development, and some protype models had been constructed and flown. Finally the General Aircraft Company Limited received approval of one design and the go-ahead to build giant gliders in the Midlands.

Named the Hamilcar, the glider was of wooden construction and was of huge proportions, having a length of 68 feet and a wing area of 1,673 square feet. It weighed 7 tons and could carry a load equal to its own weight – putting 14 tons into the air. The cockpit was a massive 25 feet above the ground, equal to the height of an average-size house, and was entered by an internal ladder. A hinged nose allowed loads to pass into and out of its cavernous hull. The two pilots sat one behind the other, with telephone communication to both the tug plane and personnel being carried inside the glider. In front of the pilots was a bulletproof screen and behind them an armour-plated section. After landing, the Hamilcar's forward roll could be brought to a stop by releasing the oil pressure in the wheel-struts, causing them to telescope, allowing the Hamilcar to sink onto its flat underside. When a tank was being carried, its exhausts were connected to funnels that carried the fumes outside the glider when the tank was started up preparatory to landing; as the Hamilcar touched down, its nose swung open, the exhausts were disconnected and as it came to a stop, the tank and crew would be driven out and be instantly ready for action.

The first exercise with a Hamilcar carrying a tank had an astonishing climax. The glider overshot the runway and at 80 miles per hour headed towards some Nissen huts. The pilot was unable to release the oil pressure and the Hamilcar bounced over rough ground and crashed into one of the huts, demolishing it. The tank burst out and continued to run forward, the very surprised driver still inside it!

Because of the Hamilcar's size, the Royal Air Force decided that only the powerful Halifax planes should tow it, and only the most experienced glider pilots were trained to fly them.

Colonel Chatterton took up a Hamilcar taking the controls himself, accompanied by glider pilot Peter Cranmer. Subsequently, in his book *The Wings of Pegasus*, he wrote:

> I found the Halifax MKV and the Hamilcar at one end of the airfield. I went into the fuselage and climbed up the ladder to the cockpit and sat down. It was a strange sensation looking out at the great wingspan, which was greater than that of the Halifax. Sitting up there the Halifax looked like a toy, its engines ticking-over and the long thick towrope lying on the ground between the two aircraft. Then I got a call from the Halifax pilot, the tow rope tautened and the tug plane and glider moved across the grass, then the Hamilcar jumped, once, twice and was airborne. She handled well in the air and then the Halifax too was airborne and the whole combination was away.
>
> The flight was uneventful, we flew first to the coast, smoothly enough, then turned north-west and over Tarrant Rushton we released from the Halifax and the Hamilcar was in free flight, with the wind swishing past the cockpit. She was so light to handle and we circled the airfield and turned into the wind. It seemed a steep angle of descent and then, as we levelled out, the great nose almost obscured the runway. She

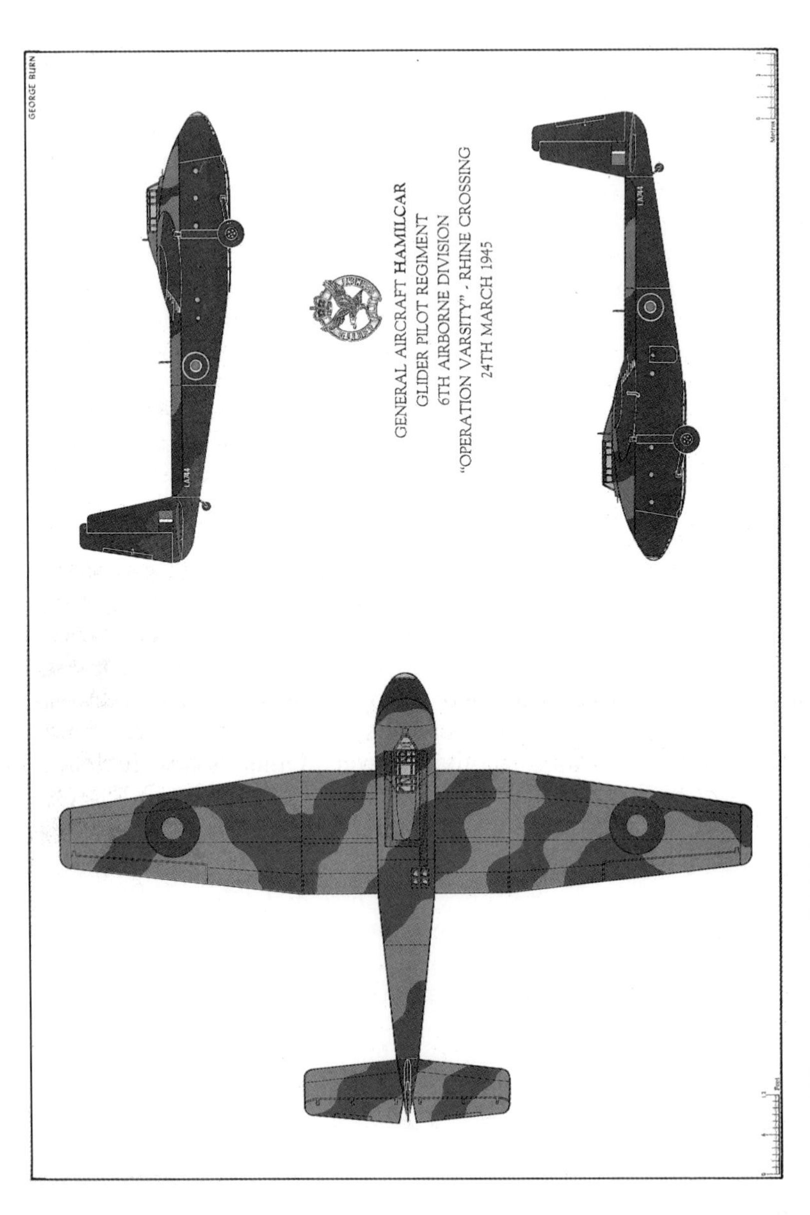

Drawn by George Burn.

floated, then settled smoothly on terra firma. I climbed down the ladder feeling a thrill of satisfaction.

A Hamilcar Squadron, based in Dorset, was formed under the command of Major A.J Dale, and it underwent an extensive training programme, the glider pilots, RAF and army airborne units all working together. Initially the Halifax crews had some qualms about towing Hamilcars fully loaded. The idea of towing 14 tons led to some apprehension, especially when it was found that the margin of airspeed between flying and stalling was only 10 miles per hour at take-off. However, both the Halifax crews and the Hamilcar pilots soon got the hang of it. Many senior officers visited Tarrant Rushton to watch the Hamilcars flying, among them the Supreme Commander, General Dwight Eisenhower, who was impressed with all he saw.

Civilians who saw the Hamilcar, with its great wingspan, huge body and bulbous nose and cockpit and massive wheels, were amazed that it could fly. More than 400 of the giant gliders were built during the war and the squadron was very active during the invasion of German-occupied Europe, carrying such loads as Tetrarch tanks, Bren-gun carriers, 25-pounder guns with ammunition and their motive power. Other loads included bridging equipment, self-propelling light anti-aircraft Bofors guns, or 40 fully-armed infantrymen. In fact the variation was enormous and the loads were always being revised and tested.

12

Italy to Yugoslavia

Operation Bunghole 1943

Following the invasion of Sicily, the main element of The Glider Pilot Regiment returned to England in November 1943, but one squadron was renamed the Independent Squadron and was sent to Oujda, French Morocco, from where it almost immediately moved back to Sicily, to Comiso, under the command of Major Coulthard. While there the squadron was detailed to send three Horsas on a special mission to Yugoslavia, and the gliders and six pilots were despatched to Bari, Italy, from where the flight was to begin and details of the operation were revealed.

The purpose of the flight was to take a Russian military mission to the headquarters of Marshal Tito at Petrovac, Yugoslavia, and the party were to be accompanied by an SAS sergeant who would act as interpreter. The gliders were to be towed by American Air Force Dakotas, but the American pilots were unhappy, believing that the Dakotas lacked the power to tow Horsas across the Adriatic Sea and over mountains to the destination. The result was that the Horsas were substituted by the smaller American Wacos, but still to be piloted by British pilots of The Glider Pilot Regiment.

In turn, the glider pilots realised that only the very best navigators would be good enough to get the combinations to their objective, so the RAF supplied three of their top navigators to fly with the Dakotas and to navigate the combinations to Petrovac in the foothills of the Dinaric Alps. To mislead the Germans a diversionary bombing raid was laid on to attack an area of Yugoslavia where it was known that there was a large concentration of enemy forces. The raid took place during the flight of the Dakota–Waco combinations and drew German fighter planes away from them.

Tito's headquarters were in an area that was snow-covered and entailed flying over the Dinaric Alps. Conferring together before the flight began, the six glider pilots, Captain Turner, Staff Sergeants Morrison and McCulloch, and Sergeants Hall, Newman and McMillan, agreed that the deep snow at their journey's end could cause landing problems and even disaster. It was considered that landing at speed, the gliders were likely to be brought to a sudden stop in the deep snow and that perhaps the noses of the gliders would dig in and cause the gliders' tails to lift, turning the gliders over. It was agreed therefore that the safest method would be to make tail-down landings; thus the tails would act as brakes and slow them down, allowing the gliders to sink gently onto the snow. Their considered decision was based on the difference in construction between the Horsa and the Waco. The former had an undercarriage that could be jettisoned to allow a landing to be made on a long skid, whereas the Waco had a fixed undercarriage and only two small skids.

The distance to be flown from Bari to the Yugoslavian coast was 150 miles, plus a further 100 miles across the Dinaric Alps, through heavy mist, to Petrovac; but the three RAF navigators did a spot-on job and took the three combinations directly over the landing zone, where they circled around looking for a thinning of the mist. When it came, a large hammer and sickle design could be seen on the ground, cut out of the snow, together with smoke signals rising towards them. Captain Turner landed first, followed by Staff Sergeants McCulloch and Morrison, together with their second pilots. Each glider made a perfect landing, to be greeted by Tito's partisans. The gliders were then burned to destroy all traces of them and the pilots were given accommodation in the homes of partisans until the time came for their return to Bari. In preparation for that day, a rough runway was made on the snow and a Dakota was flown in by British Air Commodore Whitney Straight to take the glider pilots back to Bari, from where they then travelled to Comiso to rejoin the squadron.

13

Operation Overlord

The invasion of German-occupied Europe, 6 June 1944

Introduction

The invasion of Normandy was the greatest combined operation ever undertaken. The first brief communiqué released to the British and American publics on the morning of 6 June 1944, merely stated: 'Allied naval forces supported by strong air forces, began landing Allied armies this morning on the northern coast of France.'

The deliberately vague report referred to thousands of bombers and fighter aircraft, more than 4,000 vessels and landing craft, and a million men; and, by D-Day plus 20, some 200,000 tanks and other vehicles had been landed and a huge artificial harbour, called Mulberry, had been towed across the English Channel to the French coastal area in sections, assembled while under attack, and put in place.

Five factors contributed to the brilliant success of the operation: the close co-operation between President Franklin D. Roosevelt of the USA and Winston Churchill, Prime Minister of Great Britain, the administration of General Dwight D. Eisenhower; the battle commander genius of General Bernard Montgomery, (as he was then) who led the landing force (the British 2nd Army and US 1st Army, otherwise called 21st Army Group), an outstanding set of unit commanders; and the courage of the ordinary soldiers, seamen and aircrews. A sixth factor was a *coup de main* carried out by glider pilots and a company of the Oxfordshire and Buckinghamshire Light Infantry, some seven hours ahead of the main invasion. But more of that later.

Nothing like the invasion had ever been planned before and will perhaps, never be seen again. Both Eisenhower and Montgomery knew that 'Overlord' simply had to be a success. They had seen a small-scale ill-prepared and ill-led landing at Dieppe fail, and a larger landing at Anzio, Italy had been within a hair's breadth of failing before eventually succeeding.

Should the landings have failed, the war would have been seriously prolonged and might even have resulted in the Americans dropping atom bombs on German cities, making Europe the scene of the first-ever nuclear atack, with unimaginable consequences. The effects of a failed 'Overlord' would also have been felt in the Mediterranean, and the plan to land an army in the south of France would have been abandoned. In Italy, Rome had fallen to the Allies on 4 June, two days before D-Day, but General Alexander, Commander-in-Chief in Italy, was short of both men and weapons and might have had no alternative other than to curtail his offensive. Further East, the British might have been compelled to give up trying to save Greece. Failure of 'Overlord' might also have caused the Americans to back-pedal on defeating Japan in the Far East. Additionally, the failure of 'Overlord' would have almost certainly reduced Britain to becoming a very junior member of Allied planning strategy, whereas at the time of 'Overlord', Britain was undoubtedly a leading power.

The date originally chosen for D-Day was 5 June 1944, but bad weather delayed Operation Overlord for 24 hours. But an audacious *coup de main* attack on two important bridges in Normandy actually started on the night before D-Day. This was Operation Deadstick, and involved six Horsa gliders carrying officers and men of the Oxfordshire and Buckinghamshire Regiment and the Royal Engineers.

14

Operation Deadstick

5–6 June 1944

James Wallwork remembers his first sight of a Horsa after graduating from Hotspur gliders. He said, 'I fell in love with it from the moment I first saw it. I was impressed by its size, it looked like a great black crow and from the moment that I went into the cockpit, sat in the pilot's seat and saw the size of the flaps and felt the controls, I was hooked.' In late 1943 he learned that he was to train with others for an operation in Europe, but the details were not disclosed.

Then Operation Deadstick, planned by General Gale, Commander of 6th Airborne Division, began to take shape. The general, in the knowledge that his division was to provide protection for the flank of the invasion participants, decided that two bridges, over the Caen Canal and the River Orne, should be captured by a small glider-borne force and held until the later arrival of the main invasion force. It was essential that the bridges be taken intact so that they could be used by the advancing seaborne troops. It was known that the bridges were guarded by German troops and that charges had been placed under them for demolition, if necessary.

General Gale was reluctant to give the task of attacking, taking and holding the bridges to the Parachute Brigade. He was sure that they could, but he reasoned that a parachute drop is comparatively slow, with the risk of the men dropped becoming

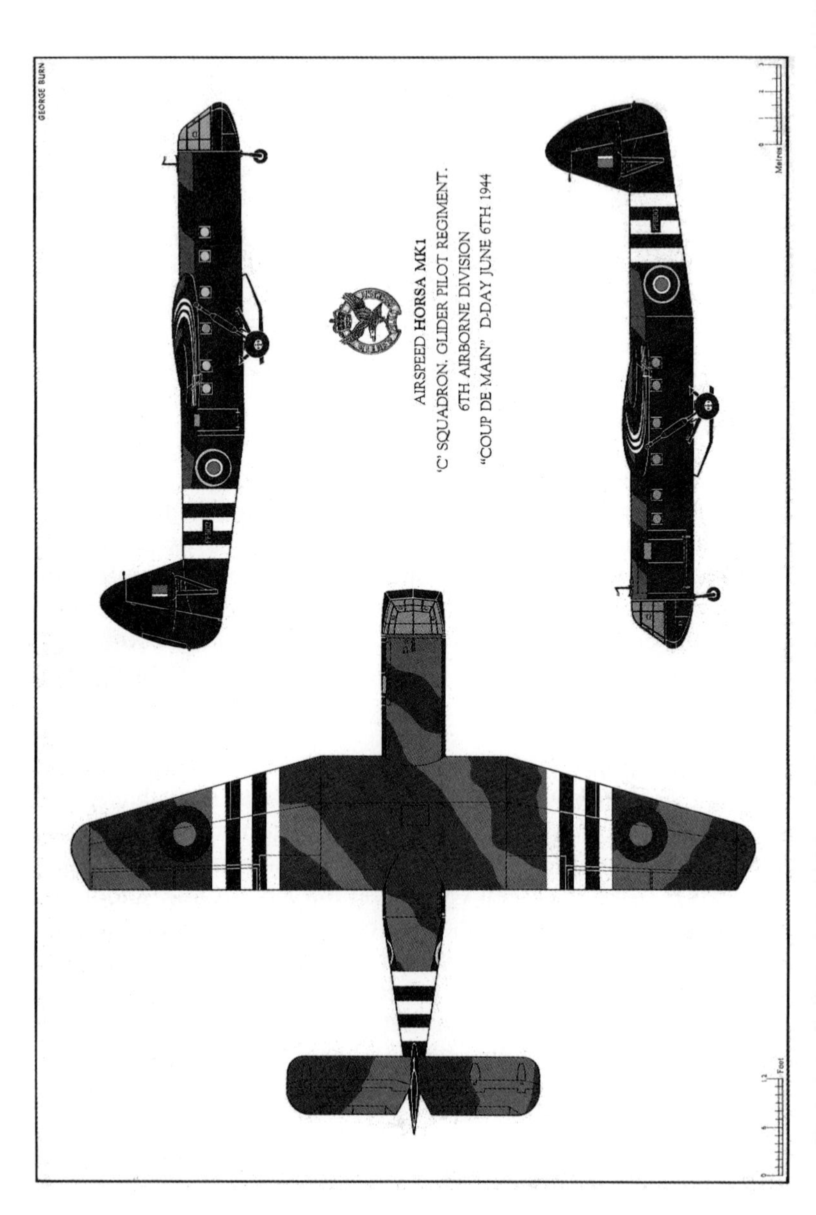

Drawn by George Burn.

scattered and needing time to regroup. He decided therefore on a *coup de main* attack and seizure by gliders, arriving silently by night and each setting down 28 well-trained, fully armed fighting men. Those pilots and men could then hold the bridges until the arrival of the Parachute Brigade.

Major John Howard, commanding D Company, the Oxfordshire and Buckinghamshire Regiment, was chosen to lead the attack. Without locations being divulged, Howard was given the essence of the task his men and the glider pilots would be given. He was sworn to secrecy but began immediately to put his company through the most intensive training. They took part in an exercise, with two bridges close enough together to simulate the company's ultimate task. Because of the demolition charges at the bridges in Normandy, General Gale also chose Captain Neilson, Royal Engineers, to select 30 sappers to join him on secondment to D Company. Each of the sappers was also a trained parachutist who would willingly have jumped into action, but to a man they objected to being flown in gliders. Their objections were eventually overcome and they began to train with Howard and his infantrymen, carrying out further exercises together.

The essence of the *coup de main* would be the ability of the glider pilots to land their Horsas close enough to the bridges. Twelve pilots were to be used, two for each of the six gliders flying the toops on the eve of D-Day, plus four reserves. They were posted to an RAF airfield at Tarrant Rushton, Dorset, where there were squadrons of Halifax bombers and a squadron of Horsa gliders. The glider pilots were all experienced and they were very well looked after, in every way.

Essex-born Roy Howard recalls, 'We had our own sleeping quarters, good food and indeed, everything we wanted. Our tug crews were billeted near to us and we worked and socialised with each other. That was a novel experience, as never before had we been so much of a team with tug pilots and crews.' Roy had joined The Glider Pilot Regiment from the Royal Corps of Signals and early in his service he became one of the official escort and firing party at the military funeral of Colonel John Rock, the regiment's first commanding officer, following his fatal crash in 1942. Late in 1943 he was teamed with Fred Baacke, who was to be his second pilot.

Training for Operation Deadstick included remote release at 6,000 feet and spot landings at night with no lights on the tug aircraft and none on the ground. That special training was for the capture of the bridges at night. Eventually, as the date for D-Day became known, the 12 pilots of the *coup de main* operation were selected. In addition to Howard and Baacke, the others were: Wallwork and Ainsworth, Barkway and Boyle, Lawrence and Shorter, Pearson and Guthrie, Boland and Hobbs. In addition to the officers and men of the Ox and Bucks and the Royal Engineers, an officer of the 7th Parachute Battalion and two Royal Army Medical Corps officers were assigned to three of the gliders. The RAF tug plane pilots were Wing Commander Duder, Flying Officers Clapperton and Archibald, and Warrant Officers Berry, Herman and Bain.

The operation began at 2220 hours on the night preceding D-Day, some seven hours ahead of the main seaborne landings on the Normandy beaches. The operation called for an early start, so that the Germans would not realise that the invasion had begun. A blind-flying approach had to be made, with a gyrocompass and stopwatch added to the standard Horsa instruments to assist the pilots make spot landings from a height of 6,000 feet over the coast of Normandy. As a decoy measure, the Halifax tugs each carried some bombs, and after the gliders released they flew on and dropped the bombs on a Caen factory. That action drew the German sound locating and radar defences with them and maximised the chances of the gliders' achieving complete surprise.

Major Howard travelled in the glider piloted by Wallwork and Ainsworth, accompanied by his leader of 24 platoon, Lieutenant D. Brotheridge, and 21 men plus 5 sappers. Lieutenant Wood and 22 men, plus Captain Neilson, RE, and 4 sappers were carried in the Horsa of pilots Boland and Hobbs; and Lieutenant Smith with 22 men of 14 platoon, plus Captain Vaughan, RAMC, and 5 sappers, flew with Staff Sergeants Barkway and Boyle. Those three gliders were to land by the bridge over the Caen Canal.

In the Horsas bound for the River Orne bridge, glider pilots Lawrence and Shorter carried Captain Priday, Howard's second in command, with Lieutenant Hooper and 21 men of 22 Platoon, plus 5 sappers. In number 5 glider, piloted by Pearson and Guthrie, were 21 men, also Lieutenant McDonald, of 7th Para, and 5 sappers and in number 6 Horsa, piloted by Howard and Baacke, were Lieutenant Fox and 21 men of 23 Platoon, together with 5 sappers.

As the leading Horsa crossed the English Channel, Oliver Boland thought of the months of training that had prepared everyone for Operation Deadstick and he knew that, to a man, everyone was alert and eager for the coming attack on the bridge and he hoped that their physical fitness and training would see them through. Major Howard recalled how the officers and men, in the hours before take-off, had checked and rechecked their personal weapons, cleaning them until the barrels shone inside. While awaiting the order to go, those that could had rested and eaten, others had played cards or written letters. One man in each platoon had a radio set strapped to his chest and each man had either a rifle, Bren, or Sten gun and ammunition, and all carried a number of grenades. The arms and ammunition each carried meant that he weighed 250 pounds, and many shoulders drooped under the weight they carried.

Jim Wallwork and John Ainsworth, in the leading Horsa, number 667, crossed the English Channel towed by Halifax 3359 of 298 Squadron. Approaching the landing zone, Wing Commander Duder, piloting the Halifax, wished them luck, and Wallwork released at 6,000 feet, about 7 miles from Bénouville, steering by compass. The two glider pilots looked for the canal and then Wallwork took the Horsa down, swooping silently alongside the waterway until he saw the bridge looming up in the darkness, the ground seeming to rush up towards them. There was barbed wire ahead and Wallwork was struggling to control the moment when the Horsa would touch down. When it did, it was doing 90 miles per hour – too fast; so he called to Ainsworth to stream the arrester chute fitted to the rear of the glider. When it opened up, the glider's nosewheel went down and the tail went up. It then bounced into the air and its wheels were torn off, but the chute checked the glider's forward speed somewhat and Ainsworth pressed the button to jettison the chute. Back on the ground, the Horsa threw up friction sparks from the rough ground and in the fuselage Major Howard thought they were tracer bullets. 'Then,' said the major, 'there was a God Almighty crash, the glider's nose was deep into the barbed wire and the front of the cockpit broke, throwing both pilots out.' Inside the glider, Major Howard and Lieutenant Brotheridge got the men out and moving quickly towards the bridge. Jim Wallwork had set 25 Platoon down exactly where it should have been, and the Germans defending the bridge had been completely surprised by the silent approach. The time was 0014 on 6 June, D-Day. Glider pilot John Ainsworth had broken a leg and a Bren gunner was drowned.

A minute later, Horsa number 661, piloted by Oliver Boland, with Philip Hobbs, landed so close behind that Boland had to swerve to avoid the other glider. Quickly Lieutenant Wood and his platoon left the glider and went forward to join the others at the bridge. By that time the enemy had become alerted and a few rifle shots had been fired from trenches at the near side of the road. The Ox and Bucks began to clear the trenches just as the third Horsa landed with a tremendous crash, and Lieutenant Smith and the men of 14 Platoon, with glider pilots Barkway and Boyle, rushed forward to join the others. The Royal Engineers went below the bridge to defuse the demolition charges, but in fact found that the German commander had failed to set any.

The sentry at the far end of the bridge fired a flare and was immediately killed by a blast from an automatic weapon. Grenades were tossed through pillbox apertures, but Germans manning machine-gun emplacements opened fire. Lieutenant

Brotheridge, running across the bridge – the first of the attackers to do so – threw a grenade at a machine-gun but was hit in the neck by a German bullet just as his grenade exploded on the machine-gun, and other infantrymen knocked out the remaining machine-guns. Brotheridge's wound was fatal and he died before Captain Vaughan reached him.

A few hundred yards east of the canal bridge was the River Orne, and it was to a bridge spanning it that the other three Horsas were heading. The objective was nearer to the coast than that at the canal, so the three gliders needed to lose their height quickly after releasing at 6,000 feet, and the Halifaxes towing them went on to drop bombs on a Caen factory. Having less distance to fly to their objective, the glider pilots had to apply full flaps, making navigation more difficult. In the normal way, full flaps were not applied until after the place at which the glider was to land came into view, and then not until the final approach. To descend at an angle of 45 degrees in the dark, at a rate of 2,000 feet per minute, whilst navigating on various courses, required great skill and strong nerves.

Charles Thornton, a sergeant with 17 Platoon, D Company, the Oxfordshire and Buckinghamshire Light Infantry, was being flown in Horsa number 664 piloted by Staff Sergeant Roy Howard and second pilot Sergeant Fred Baacke. He recalls, 'We had been training by night and day for the operation to capure the River Orne bridge. Everything depended on split-second timing and maximum speed. Then, having captured it, we had to hold it until the Allied forces arrived from the beaches in the morning. As we glided in over France, with the Horsa descending, it began dipping and Roy Howard, the pilot, was pulling his control column back as hard as he could. He shouted to Lieutenant Fox, our platoon leader, to move two or three men from the front to the back. The Horsa hit the ground at 90 miles per hour but amazingly we got out unharmed. It was 0019 hours. The invasion force would not be on the beaches for about another seven hours. The Royal Engineers with us went under the bridge and reported that no charges had been set.'

Roy Howard remembers that their objective was revealed three days before the mission, when the glider pilots were shown, on a sand table, a precise model of the terrain around their destination, detailed to the last tree. They knew little of any grand plan, but what they did learn from the sand table was that the gliders were to land near Caen. Roy's glider was to be the last of three to land in a specific corner of a particular tiny field of rough pasture. He knew that if he undershot he would destroy his seven tons of powerless aircraft and its human cargo on a belt of 50-foot-high trees at one end of the field; and, if he overshot, all would be crushed against a 40-foot-high embankment that carried the road at the other end. This was a not unreasonable task in broad daylight, but daunting in the pitch-black of midnight, with no more than a few yards either way available for error.

'As I walked to my Horsa to begin the historic flight I had no particular awareness of embarking on a feat of navigation and airmanship that had not been attempted before and which to my knowledge, has not been tried since. Such was the intensity of my training that I was thinking only of the job in hand.

'As we sat inside our beautifully made Horsa, inhaling the overpowering, but not unpleasant smell of new wood and casein glue, the first three gliders took off, rumbling on their wheels at the end of two hundred and seventy-five-foot ropes behind the Halifax bomber tugs, bound for Pegasus Bridge. They were to take a longer route and to land simultaneously with us, just a few hundred yards away. We took off at two-minute intervals; I was the last of the six, airborne at one minute past eleven.

'Our tug gradually turned us away from the sunset, and we crossed the coast near Worthing, heading to a more southerly horizon that was pitch-dark, allowing our eyes to adjust to night vision. We saw no other aircraft but our own Halifax tug at the front of our umbilical line; we even lost sight of that on several brief occasions as we passed through cloud, causing a momentary flutter of worry. To steer a proper course, the glider pilot needs to keep his tug in constant view.

'As midnight approached, Paddy O'Shea, the tug navigator, gave us a compass reading over the intercom and informed us that we were on course, about three miles from the French coast.

' "OK, you're there," announced Paddy over the intercom, "go when you like." We had, in fact, to go that very instant; split-second timing was essential, for from this moment we would be on our own, guided through the dark only by our own powerless wings and by compass heading and stopwatch. I released the towline and the roar of air past our wooden aircraft gradually died to a hiss as our speed began to fall. The Halifax had released us at six thousand feet and had then continued directly ahead to attack its target, in order to delude any watching enemy into thinking that we were part of a normal bombing raid on Caen rather than participants in a daring *coup de main* which relied entirely on surprise. The noisy metal Halifax would take all the enemy's radar and sound location devices with it whilst we dropped silently to earth.

'And therein lay the difficulty of the navigational task that now faced us. From that height a Horsa would normally have glided to earth in twelve miles but my destination lay only 5 miles away and to get there I had to descend at a perilously steep forty-five degrees, slowing the craft sufficiently to avoid wild overshooting or a disastrous crash landing, and needing to make three changes of course by dead reckoning on the way. To do all that I had six minutes.

'Our tug had cast us off at a hundred and twenty mph and to reduce us to our planned gliding speed of eighty mph I immediately applied full flaps; but I realised at once that she was nose heavy, and even with the control column pulled right back against my chest I could not get her to slow below ninety mph.

'We were dropping like a streamlined brick, and I knew at once that we were not only incorrectly loaded, but overloaded. The men had clearly armed themselves with a great deal of extra ammunition and grenades, but I suspect to this day that an extra

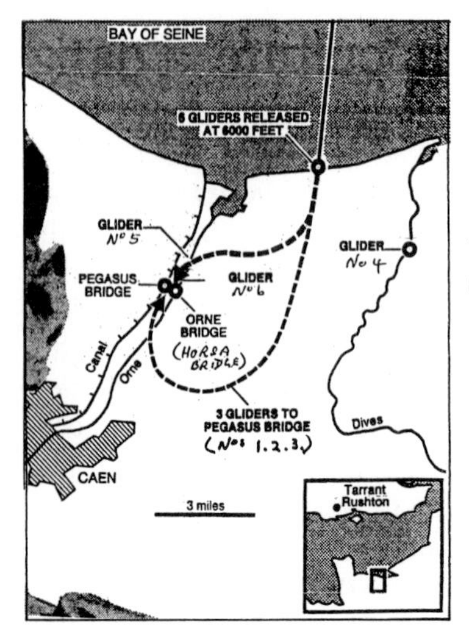

The route Roy Howard took his glider after cast off, to capture the River Orme bridge.

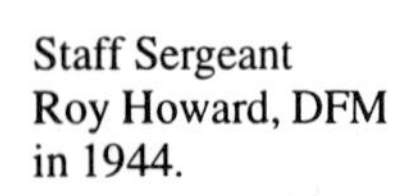

Staff Sergeant Roy Howard, DFM in 1944.

body smuggled himself aboard at the last minute; men were terribly keen to go on this mission.

' "Mr Fox!" I yelled to the lieutenant in charge of the men, "two men from the front to the back – and quickly!" It worked. Balance was restored and, once again, I had control over the aircraft.

'From the moment of casting off we were committed to landing in that one tiny field, with no room for error and no opportunity to change our minds. Ours was an almost straight descent by the shortest route, whereas the three gliders assigned to Pegasus Bridge had a gentler and lower descent, with the added luxury of circling their landing site before they went down.

'We were now back on our planned descent rate of one thousand feet per minute. We held our first course of two hundred and twelve degrees for the allotted ninety seconds, my second pilot, Freddie Baacke, guiding us by a stopwatch lit by the tiniest of hand-held lights. Then we made a turn on to two hundred and sixty-nine degrees, which we held for two minutes thirty seconds, and finally turned on two hundred and twelve degrees for the run in. At our acute angle of descent the standard compass would have been useless and we relied instead on a gyro direction indicator.

'As we made our third change of course and were down to twelve hundred feet, I could suddenly see the parallel waterways of the Caen Canal and the River Orne glistening silver in the diffused moonlight glowing from behind the clouds. A rain squall at that moment would have blotted out all our vision and might well have proved fatal. We had no windscreen wiper, and no way to abort the mission; but the whole landscape was discernible, if only just, and it looked so like the sand table model that I felt that I had been there before.

'I was afraid that we were still going down too fast, so I took off the flaps for a moment to flatten the glide path. I just managed to clear the tops of the fifty-foot trees at the beginning of our field and immediately applied the parachute brake, wheel brakes, and full flaps to prevent us careering into the embankment at the far end. There was one final, unexpected hazard: no one had mentioned that there would be a herd of cows in the field!

'I am sure we hit a cow, which knocked off our nose wheel. It was nine minutes past midnight when, with a rumble and a final clatter, I came to rest just six yards from our allotted spot, less than a hundred yards from our objective of the bridge. There was the briefest moment of silence.

' "You're in the right place, sir," I announced to a pleasantly surprised Lieutenant Fox, and before I could even leave my seat, he and his men had flung open the door and alighted in a stampede of boots. I was aghast to observe that, of the two other gliders which should have landed before me, there was no sign: the force that had set out to capture the Orne Bridge was thus a mere third of the size that it should have been. Nevertheless, within fifteen minutes, it was indeed captured.

'I subsequently learned that the second glider had landed short, but safely, in another field four hundred yards behind us and the first, because of an error by its tug navigator, had landed by the wrong bridge, on the wrong river, ten miles away. But they captured that bridge and, with great courage, then fought their way back to where they should have been.

'The night was full of noise and alarms, culminating in the ear-shattering barrage that preceded the first dawn seaborne landings. Sitting in our slit trenches, we listened as the barrage from the armada of ships swept slowly up from the beaches and we hoped that someone would remember that we were there and would stop the torrent of shells and rockets before they reached us and the two bridges. Fortunately, it stopped in time.

'At one-thiry a.m. paratroopers arrived to reinforce our perimeter, and twelve hours later Lord Lovat and his commandos reached us from the beaches.'

The bridge over the River Orne was re-named 'Horsa Bridge' and Staff Sergeant Roy Howard's part in the successful operation won him the Distinguished Flying Medal.

Once the bridge had been taken, 17 Platoon were soon reinforced by 23 Platoon, led by Lieutenant 'Tod' Sweeney, who had flown in the 5th Horsa, piloted by Staff Sergeant Stanley Pearson, which had landed in another field further away.

After 23 Platoon left the Horsa, Lieutenant Sweeney led his men towards the bridge at a trot. With them went Lieutenant McDonald, the 7 Para's liaison officer, and, with pilots Pearson and Guthrie, they had about 400 yards to cover. Sweeney recalls, 'When we reached the bridge there was no opposition and I realised that we were not the first to have arrived. I left a section at the west bank and crossed over the bridge with the other two sections, and on the other side saw Lieutenant Fox and his men. The calm and the lack of action came as an anticlimax.'

By 20 minutes after midnight Major Howard's men had secured the canal bridge; all resistance from the slit trenches and machine-gun emplacements had been overcome, many Germans had been killed and others had run away. The Ox and Bucks did not take prisoners – it was a case of anything that moved being shot or blown up with grenades. Lieutenant Wood was hit by several bullets in his legs, and another subaltern, Sandy Smith, had his wrist smashed. Jim Wallwork, the pilot of the first glider to land, was hit while carrying ammunition from the Horsa to the troops at the bridge. Captain Jack Neilson and his sappers, after examining the bridge for explosives had joined the others in an infantry role. With three platoon leaders killed or wounded, NCOs had taken command of the platoons.

Although pleased with the way things had gone, Major Howard did not know whether the attack on the river bridge had been successful and he wondered how Captain Priday, his second in command, was getting on. Then his radio operator picked up a message from the Orne group, 'We have captured the bridge.'

Howard immediately passed the news to his men at the canal bridge, and his radio operator was sending a success call towards where the paras were, hoping that it would be picked up by them.

Captain Priday and Lieutenant Hooper, in Horsa 662, piloted by Lawrence and Shorter, had been taken by their tug plane to a wrong point of release, and when Lawrence cast off he flew inland until he saw a river below him. It was not until they were on the ground that they realised it was the wrong river and bridge – it was the River Dives, 10 miles from their real objective. However, they attacked and killed the bridge defenders and then, by compass, set out to travel the 10 miles to join D Company, fighting their way as they went. It was a tremendous and courageous effort.

Captain Vaughan, RAMC, had set up an aid post to attend to the wounded, and Major Howard sent a signal to the Orne bridge asking for a platoon to be sent to him. Lieutenant Fox marched 17 Platoon the 400 yards across to the canal bridge, taking an anti-tank PIAT with them. As they marched they could hear the rumbling of tanks in the direction of the canal bridge. On arrival Sergeant Thornton was sent, with the PIAT, to take up his position at a T-junction on the far side of the bridge.

At the canal bridge troops had made contact with the owners of the bar-café at the western end. Georges and Thérèse Gondrée had, for many years, supplied the Allies with bits of information gleaned from German officers and men who had patronised the establishment. Georges was so delighted that the British had arrived that he went into the garden and dug up some bottles of champagne he had buried before the Germans arrived four years earlier. The two adult Gondrées and their two small daughters made the airborne troops welcome.

At the T-junction Charlie Thornton could hear two tanks moving nearby. It was 0145 when he saw the tanks appear, stop, and the two tank commanders get out and hold a conversation. Thornton prepared for action as the first tank moved towards him. He aimed his PIAT, pressed the trigger and scored a hit on the tank. The ammunition inside the tank – machine-gun bullets, grenades and shells – was all set off. 'There was an enormous explosion,' recalls Charles Thornton, 'and bits and pieces flew everwhere, lighting up the darkness with a sort of fireworks display. The second tank turned round and disappeared into the distance.'

In the café-bar, Thérèse Gondrée was kissing and hugging the troops, their blackened camouflaged faces blackening hers. Georges was busily opening bottles of champagne. Arlette and Georgette, his children, were only small but now, married to an Englishman, Arlette recalls the arrival of the gliders and the troops they carried, and how they arrived at the café and were welcomed by her parents. 'Daddy looked from an upper window and saw figures moving and heard English voices. Then some British soldiers, with blackened faces and wearing steel helmets, entered the café-bar and Lieutenant Dan Thomas of the Oxfordshire and Buckinghamshire Light Infantry sat me on his knee and gave me a piece of chocolate, the first I had ever had. More soldiers arrived and ever since then we have traditionally opened champagne for returning veterans on anniversary days. I remember the wounded being brought into the café and how my mother helped to nurse them.

'During the German occupation my mother, who spoke German but never admitted to it, used to pick up information, which she gave to my father, who spoke English. In his turn, he passed the information to Madam Vion, a director of the local maternity hospital, who worked for the Resistance, who passed information to the Allies.

'My father died in 1969, and my mother in 1984, and since then I have run the café. Now, sadly, the bridge has been pulled down by the authorities to make room for a new one, and the pieces of the old bridge now lie on a nearby caravan site, but the café and the area is designated a National Monument.'

After four years' training with 7th Parachute Battalion, Captain

Richard Todd, a film actor who later starred in the film *The Dam Busters* recalls his experiences after his battalion landed in Normandy 30 minutes after the glider pilots taking part in the *coup de main.* Their brief was to reinforce the airborne troops who had captured and were holding the two bridges over the River Orne and the Caen Canal and to establish the western bridgehead that would protect 6th Airborne's west flank, and prevent counter-attacking German forces from moving out of the Caen area. At all costs the western bridgehead was to hold firm until relieved by forward elements of the 3rd Division, late on D-Day afternoon.

Todd remembers: 'As I was jumping number one, I straddled the end of a coffin-shaped hole. As the Stirling crossed the Normandy coast I saw yellowy-orange dots coming up towards us and as the normal loading of tracer was one in every five bullets, I realised there was a lot of lead flying about.

'At about 0040 on Tuesday, 6th June 1944, I landed in a cornfield in Normandy, an illegal immigrant without a passport, but welcome, I hoped, at least to the locals.

'Taking stock I saw aircraft still coming in and I got my bearings from their flight path. There was no one near me and I knew that it was because I had jumped number one and therefore the others would be beyond me. To the east I could make out the darker shape of a wood about 800 metres distant; the dropping zone was being raked by small-arms fire, so I decided to get into the wood. I put my Sten gun together and loaded it. In a clearing in the woods I found my commanding officer, Colonel Pine-Coffin, and about a dozen others and hoped that the colonel's name was not an omen of things to come.

'The CO said there was no way of knowing whether the glider-borne atttack on the bridges had been successful and we must get there as soon as possible. We broke out of the woods and set off at the double. By about 0100 our group had grown to about fifty and we stopped to rendezvous. Half an hour later the CO gave the order to move off to the bridges. Our numbers had grown to a hundred and fifty, about a quarter of our strength. Just then glider pilot Boland appeared, to lead us to the bridges that had already been captured by the glider-borne troops.

'We doubled along the causeway towards the canal bridge, a large iron structure that could be opened to allow the passage of seagoing vessels. Suddenly, all hell erupted on the road ahead. Heavy explosions, colourful flashes and tracer rent the sky like a spectacular fireworks display. This is it. Here we go! I thought. We increased the speed of our jog-trot then, suddenly, the tumult died down. An MKA tank, probing the bridgehead, had been hit by a PIAT bomb fired by a sergeant with the glider-borne force, causing its ammunition to explode.

'We reached the café-bar at the west end of the bridge and Pine-Coffin directed me to set up battalion HQ three hundred metres further on, below the village of Le Port, whose church was on the crest. From there I had a perfect view over the bridges and into the divisional area. In the distance, beyond the River Orne the sky was stippled with flashes and smoke from explosions or air-burst shells. In the foreground was the canal bridge, so brilliantly captured a few hours before by the glider-borne force. By our end of the bridge stood the bar-café owned by the Gondrée family. It was now a first-aid post.

'Already fastened to the canal bridge was a roughly painted sign: "PEGASUS BRIDGE", a name derived from the badge worn by British airborne forces – the winged horse of mythology.'

Oliver Boland, the number two pilot of the first Horsa to land, went off towards Caen. He later returned, leading a group of 7th Battalion paras who had not found the bridge. 'The paras were supposed to relieve us,' says Boland, ' but I had to go out to find them and bring them in.'

A crew member of the Halifax that towed Horsa number 5 for its landing by the River Orne, was Walter Wright, who related:

'Towards midnight on 5th June 1944, we were towing one of three gliders carrying men of the Airborne Division, to make landings close to the bridge spanning the River Orne, seven miles inland from the coast. The troop's mission was to capture the bridge and hold it as a vital link for the land forces who would follow up from landings on Normandy beaches. As we were returning to England our Halifax shuddered, then caught fire and went down into the sea. We had been hit by a German shell. Within minutes the six of us, crew of the Halifax, were in the sea watching our dinghy sink. It had been badly holed by the same shell. We linked arms for added buoyancy and trod water for two hours until picked up by a passing minesweeper.'

Major Howard, badly wounded in the legs and hip, was later invalided from the army. A regular officer, his wound brought an end to his miltary career.

An audacious operation, carried out by Horsa gliders, and completed before the arrival of paratroops and some eight hours ahead of the main seaborne landings on the Normandy beaches, on D-Day, it paved the way for the success of the Allied invasion of Europe.

For all the survivors it had been a day to remember.

Much has been written of the daring glider operation to capture the Pegasus Bridge over the Caen Canal, but some authors have chosen to ignore the parallel mission to take the River Orne Bridge nearby, although, as Roy Howard's account reveals, the Orne operation required an even greater degree of flying skill, and one with a considerably higher risk of failure; for once cast off from the towing aircraft the die was cast and there could be no second chance.

Staff Sergeant James Wallwork, DFM.

15

D-Day

Other glider operations

While the assaults on the Canal and River Orne bridges were taking place more gliders took off, carrying close support weapons for parachutists. The gliders and their tug planes experienced a lot of air turbulence and when the Horsas made their landings in the dark several of them crashed into vertical anti-invasion poles erected by the Germans. Despite this, the loads being carried were all salvaged and afterwards the glider pilots fought on the ground as infantry, with great courage. Six Horsas reached the Normandy coast 30 minutes after midnight on 6 June. Although four of these failed to reach their target, having been released in the wrong place, the other two arrived safely, the pilots delivering their loads successfully before joining the infantry.

A vital target of the D-Day operations was the Merville battery, an oval shaped group of four massive concrete gun emplacements with heavy guns facing the coast. These emplacements were surrounded by barbed wire, an anti-tank ditch and a minefield. The Germans believed it to be impregnable. It was imperative that the gun emplacements should be destroyed as their guns were trained towards the beach on which the 3rd Division would land at dawn.

The 9th Parachute battalion, under Lieutenant Colonel Otway had the unenviable job of destroying this battery, supported by gliders carrying jeeps, light guns, Bangalore torpedoes, mortars, mine detectors and shock troops. The construction of the emplacements with their guns and German troops made the 9th Paras task a formidable one, whilst the combination of the wire, anti-tank ditch and minefields posed a difficult problem for the glider pilots.

The plan to destroy the battery was elaborate. Lancaster bombers were to attack with heavy bombs before the ground troops went in. The paratroops, together with glider-borne troops, would make the assault, and the final surprise was to have three gliders land directly on top of the battery. There would be barely an hour to complete the mission. The Royal Navy was to simultaneously bombard the battery from the sea in advance of the 3rd division landing on the beach at dawn. In the event, the RAF air strike failed as not a single bomb fell on the target.

The paras rendezvoused in the dark at Varaville, but the glider pilots had to land on, or very close to the Merville battery itself. In poor visibility the pilots and navigators of the tug planes mistook the town of Merville for the battery, which was further inland, and of a dozen Horsas carrying crucial equipment for the assault only five landed close to the battery after negotiating a landing zone thickly planted with vertical anti-invasion poles.

Paratroops dropped widely apart over a great distance, and out of a battalion strength of 700 only 100 made rendezvous with Colonel Otway. This small band of men then had to cut through 9-foot-thick barbed wire barricades and crawl in the moonlight across the approaches to the battery, feeling for trip wires and prodding the ground to avoid exploding land mines, until they reached positions from which they awaited the order to attack.

Meanwhile, Staff Sergeant Bone carried 26 volunteer assault troops in a Horsa which had been fitted with an 'arrester chute' at the rear end. While flying over the English Channel, air turbulence caused it to stream out, the resulting drag on the tug plane almost causing it to stall. The tug pilot was forced to lose

Horsa gliders after landings N.E. of Caen. The fuselages can be seen detached from the wings and nose section to facilitate quick unloading.

D-Day, 6th June 1944. Gliders and tug planes lined up at Tarrant Rushden, Dorset, ready for take-off.

height over Normandy, descending to only 1,000 feet and as no-one could see any kind of objective in the dark, he put on his landing lights while making several cirular flights over the area. This of course alerted the garrison and both tug and glider were struck by anti-aircraft fire. Although both aircraft eventually landed within only 100 yards of the guns, they immediately came under heavy machine gun attack, preventing the assault troops from reaching the battery.

Staff Sergeant Stanley Kerr found his glider flying in thick fog over the Normandy coast and his tug plane took him down to 1,000 feet to get below it. That action robbed Kerr of his planned remote release and the tug pilot therefore took him on to the battery position. Neither Kerr, nor his co-pilot Sergeant Walker, was able to see the target in the dark, so the tug plane made six runs across the area. Both tug and glider were repeatedly fired upon by the enemy, but the Horsa released and landed only the length of a cricket pitch from the emplacements. The pilots and the men they had carried were immediately subjected to an attack on the ground with automatic weapons. Although both the tug and glider had been hit several times and some of the assault troops were wounded, the remaining men were able to join up with the 9th Parachute Battalion. Staff Sergeant Kerr was subsequently awarded the Distinguished Flying Medal.

While these men were moving towards the target some RAF Lancasters began dropping 400 pound bombs, so the attacking troops took cover in a ditch. When things eventually quietened down, Captain Hudson of the Paras led them across barbed wire defences beneath the outlines of the four large seaward-pointing guns. Machine guns opened up from three different points. A company sergeant major with the assault party silenced two of them while his men managed to take out the third. Glider pilot Dixon saw Captain Hudson gravely wounded.

The three gliders that were to land troops directly on top of the battery had arrived overhead and were looking for the pre-arranged signal, a star-shaped shell fired from a mortar. However, there was no mortar available and the troops on the ground could only watch helplessly as the gliders circled above them, silhouetted against the moonlight and gradually losing height as they came under attack. Eventually they did land and the glider pilots joined the troops they had carried, fighting on the ground as they moved towards the objective. Soon afterwards the men manning the German battery surrendered and the assault party then destroyed the guns just as the 3rd Division began to land.

The 1st Airborne Armoured Reconnasissance Regiment, all volunteers, had exercised extensively with the Glider Pilot Regiment in the months before D-Day, and were thrilled to be introduced to the Hamilcars that were to carry their Tetrarch tanks and crews. As Lieutenant Watson recalls they had several flights in them at Tarrant Rushton where they also underwent intensive briefings for the Merville operation. He remembers:

'The Paras had gone in first and, assisted by special assault troops, augmented by the pilots of the gliders that flew them, had captured the battery, and we flew over later towed by specially adapted Halifaxes. Tarrant Rushton had a bump at the end of the runway and the trick was to get airborne before hitting it, otherwise there was a God Almighty bump and the glider jumped into the air!

'Crossing the English Channel, we could see hundreds of boats of all kinds and there were scores of fighter planes buzzing around us. Approaching the French coast, we got into the tank ready for landing. We got down all right and ran our tank out and into action, driving through an ambush of German machine-guns that were firing at us. We spotted where they were and put them out of action.'

Staff Sergeant Leslie Foster, crossing the French coast soon afterwards, operated his tow-rope release and both he and his co-pilot began searching for their landing zone, then put the glider's nose down. Almost immediately afterwards Foster's Horsa was in collision with another glider which soared up under it. Its undercarriage was ripped away and he had no control over the speed of the glider as it went towards the ground. The Horsa landed on its belly at 100 miles an hour in a cornfield, skidding along with the earth and corn showing through the broken floor. Ahead, Foster saw some trees and grassland. He managed to slew the Horsa round in a half circle, with the soil churning up around them. It came to a stop as a wing fell off, but miraculously no-one had been seriously hurt.

Another Horsa, piloted by Staff Sergeant Leslie Proctor and Sergeant Jim Wright, flew through tracer towards the landing area, on which there were already a great number of gliders. German gunners on the ground gave Proctor and Wright's Horsa a warm welcome and Les had to take evasive action while descending. He made a cross-wing landing among the anti-invasion poles. Proctor wrote:

'I manoeuvred the Horsa until we were flying just above the poles, then Wright applied full-flap and approaching a gap I pushed the stick forward, hard. Both wings struck poles simultaneously, and with a rending of wood we made a heavy landing, stopping before we hit other poles. The artillerymen we had carried were shaken but not injured, and with the help of Sergeant Wright they unloaded their gun and ammunition.'

While they were doing so, Les Foster began to look around but was fired upon from a church tower. Going back to the others, he took a Bren gun, sighted it, and opened fire on the church tower, quietening the sniper. The artillerymen departed and the two glider pilots set off on a compass bearing to find their rendezvous, passing on the way another Horsa that had crashed among the poles, killing both its pilots. Arriving at the rendezvous, they joined other members of 'B' Squadron and with them returned the next day to Brize Norton to prepare for another operation.

Horsa pilot Ian Muir's uneventful flight over the English Channel was a stark contrast to a dramatic and almost disastrous landing in Normandy. Having released from his tug plane, he began his

Dead soldiers and out-of-action tanks.

descent in timed changes of course, but nearing the ground enemy flak shot away a large section of his starboard wing and, out of control, the Horsa landed on top of another glider that had landed earlier. Miraculously neither Ian, his co-pilot, or their passengers were seriously injured, and fortunately those in the glider on which they landed had already departed.

At breakfast on June 6th 1944 George 'Dusty' Miller ate only a little, his mind being filled with thoughts of the coming take-off, the flight across the Channel, and his landing on enemy terrain. His lack of appetite did not, however, betray a lack of confidence: it was what he had been trained for.

Just before reaching the French coast he saw the towline between another Horsa and its tug plane part and the glider begin to lose height. As Miller released from his own tug be began to get his bearings and look for a suitable place to land. His main thoughts were on avoiding the anti-invasion poles – Rommel's asparagus, as the pilots called them. In spite of his caution his glider hit one of the poles and lost its starboard wing; the Horsa's tail unit was also damaged. Nevertheless the men of the Royal Engineers that he had been carrying were all able to disembark uninjured.

Nick Benson had been to France with the 9th Lancers in 1939, but after Dunkirk he transferred to the 6th Armoured Reconnaissance Regiment and later got his first taste of being flown in gliders. Initially there was no means of getting the Regiment's 6-ton Tetrarch tanks into the air in Horsas but the officers and crews made a number of acclimatisation flights to get them used to a new form of transport. Eventually, at Tarrant Rushton, they were introduced to the huge Hamilcar gliders and made a number of flights in them with the tanks.

'When I first saw a Hamilcar,' said Nick, 'I was amazed at its size. It was huge and beautiful and even the pilots of the specially adapted Halifaxes that towed them were initially overawed at their vastness. In spite of their qualms, they handled beautifully and I admired the skills and nonchalance of the Hamilcar pilots.

Prior to D-Day we made a number of flights with our tanks as part of our pre-invasion training and I grew to have great faith in the men at the controls of these huge, flimsy gliders.

'On D-Day our flight to Normandy was uneventful, and when the pilot of the glider announced that we were nearing our landing zone my crew and I got into our Tetrarch tank to be ready to leave as soon as we touched down. Then the Hamilcar released from the Halifax and was in free flight. It touched down, and as it came to a halt we moved forward and out of the glider and onto French soil, accelerated away and were almost immediately in action.'

Alec Ross of the *News Chronicle*, who had flown to Normandy in a Horsa described the activity before they landed: 'As we crossed the Normandy coast I went to the back of the cockpit and could see the two pilots busily engaged. As we came down from a high-tow position there was some slipstream turbulence and the pilot at the controls looked a bit strained as he struggled to hold the Horsa in level flight. Over the intercom came the tug pilot's voice advising that the release point was coming up and wishing them good luck.

'Shortly afterwards the first pilot spoke to his co-pilot, who told me to go back to my seat. As I moved to do so, he released the towrope and the glider slipped to starboard and we began to descend. I looked around at the sergeant and men of the Royal Engineers we were carrying and awaited the moment of touchdown. When it came we rolled forward and I said a silent prayer, but fortunately the pilot avoided hitting any of the anti-glider obstructions and everything went according to the textbook. Pausing to express my thanks to the pilots, I stepped down onto French soil, to the accompaniment of the chatter of machine guns, the staccato crack of small arms fire and the c-crump of artillery.'

Alec Hill, and co-pilot Bill Rossiter, carried two fully loaded jeeps with medical supplies, together with their drivers. They encountered smoke, he says, as they neared the ground and saw another Horsa hit by flak. Once down, Alec and Bill quickly got out of the glider with their rifles and kit. Their passengers did likewise, but the four men found that the jeeps and contents were trapped inside the Horsa; its tail was jammed and had to be blown off. Once the jeeps and their loads were on the ground they headed towards Ranville, where they joined others, but only after twice having to fight off German patrols.

Another large landing involved 250 gliders carrying men of the 6th Air Landing Brigade, together with their equipment and artillery. The landing zones had been cleared of obstruction poles by parachute engineers and consisted of four lanes running north and south, divided between Horsas and Hamilcars. No larger glider force had ever before been flown into battle The Hamilcars made history by flying, for the first time ever, an armoured formation into a war zone. The Light Armoured Reconnasissance Regiment, with Tetrarch tanks and Bren gun carriers, startled the enemy, with whom they made early contact.

At a re-union in Chester, some years ago, Tom Pearce, who was later closely concerned with the recovery of an incomplete Horsa and its installation as one of the first exhibits of what was later to become the Army Flying Museum, told a story of a Horsa en route to Normandy:

'Shortly before reaching the South coast the Horsa's tow rope broke and with the glider in free flight, the pilot and co-pilot began to prepare for an emergency landing. Circling around and steadily losing altitude, they searched anxiously for a suitable place to land, aware all the time of the troops and armaments being carried inside the plane. They saw a field, not large, but one that looked suitable and not too remote for them to summon help once they got down. There were houses around two sides, a church and churchyard on another. and a road running alongside the other boundary. The pilot decided to make his approach from the west to enable him to take down the Horsa between the end of the houses and the church.

'In the event he got down smoothly, but rather too fast, and the field, which proved to be the village green, was smaller than he had thought. The Horsa finished up with its nose only inches from the road, along which a convoy of armed vehicles was approaching.'

Tom also told of a mid-air crash in which he was involved: 'Crossing the coast of France, fifteen hundred feet up, it seemed almost as though we were on exercise. We released and the air was crowded with gliders, paratroops and discarded tow ropes. We went down on full flap, turning, when without warning there was a tremendous jolting crash and my glider almost stalled by colliding with another, previously unseen, glider. We were only 600 feet up, with little time to regain control.

'We landed sideways, after rushing through a cornfield and coming to a rough and jerky stop. My co-pilot and I chopped our way out of the wreckage and dashed to where the other glider had come down. The tail unit had gone, and it had dived, almost vertically, from 600 feet. All aboard were dead.'

A Horsa carrying men of the Royal Artillery was fired upon as it approached its landing area, on which other gliders had already got down; some were intact, but others were damaged or completely wrecked. George Grout, a bombardier, remembers that German gunners on the ground made the glider's approach an alarming experience and the pilot made every evasive move that he could during his approach. Just above the vertical anti-invasion poles the pilot glided in before the final descent, his co-pilot applying the flaps. Both wings of the Horsa struck poles and were torn off. The wingless glider made a heavy landing before stopping, but hit no more poles. 'My men were badly shaken up by the experience but quickly gathered themselves, unloaded and were soon able to go into action.'

Further away, a glider pilot, armed with an automatic, was stalking a sniper. He had sighted the German's position and was making his way, stealthily, until he got into position to fire at the enemy marksman. When the moment came, he killed the German instantly, but evidence of the sniper's efficiency lay around close to other gliders.

Meanwhile, Charles Roach, piloting a Horsa, was trying to control the exact instant at which his glider lost its fight with gravity. Roach could see the ground and the upright poles rushing towards him. He was flying at 90 miles an hour, but could do nothing to slow down his approach; the Horsa's flaps were not working. As the wheels touched down, the glider bounced and bounced again. The three wheels were torn off and the aircraft continued forward on its skids until its nose crumpled against one pole and its wing struck another. The glider came to a halt, and heeled over sideways. The seats inside the plane broke loose with the impact and both pilots were thrown against the perspex of the cockpit, knocking them unconscious.

Inside the Horsa the troops being carried were bruised and dazed, and some of them were knocked unconscious for a few moments. The knowledge that he was in danger gave each man an added impetus to his actions as the troops smashed their way out of the badly damaged plane. Their intensive training paid off as they made a quick exit with their weapons, ammunition and supplies. The pilots had also recovered consciousness and joined them on the ground.

Roach survived the war and when his military service came to an end, he enrolled at a theological college, was ordained and was eventually appointed to his own parish in Cornwall.

Jim Davies remembers his first shock after flying to Normandy with his platoon. 'The Horsa's approach and landing were made in the face of enemy flak but, after we had come to a stop, the pilot was remarkably cool. He was a staff sergeant named Yeoman, I think and while we unloaded he took a Bren gun and kept firing towards a place from where a ground attack from machine guns was coming. As we completed unloading the enemy fire ceased. Soon after moving off, we came across our first dead –

three German soldiers – and I thought, Oh God, they were probably conscripts like us, not professional soldiers.'

R.P. 'Henry' Ford was also flown to Normandy in a Horsa and recalls the period after the glider released;

'It was hectic, flak was bursting all around us and the pilot was taking evasive action as he descended. Just before landing there was a crash and the glider lurched violently; it had hit an anti-invasion pole. The Horsa slewed, hit another pole, then touched down; the nose dropped, and we came to a sudden stop. When we got out of the plane it was in a sorry state, minus one wing and with the other one broken. The nose was dug into the ground and the perspex in front of the cockpit was broken. Amazingly, both pilots were all right and surprisingly self-possessed and to my relief, none of the chaps with me suffered any serious injury.

'It was my first operation and I did not enjoy the experience of being shot at. It was the first time it had hit home: the Germans were trying to kill me. I had no personal axe to grind against them, and no doubt they had none against me; they were just doing what they had been trained to do. I returned fire to preserve my own life and I still feel very sorry that it was necessary to kill. I have retained, too, great admiration of the glider pilot's skill in getting me down in very difficult circumstances. Sadly, I do not know his name.'

Whatever the circumstances, any fear was subordinated among the highly trained pilots of the elite Glider Pilot Regiment. Glider pilot Robert Ashby said, 'George Chatterton always made it clear to aspiring glider pilots that they should never reveal any fear, or give way to pain. Each soldier was a commando-type fighter on the ground and a skilled pilot, able to fly several different types of aircraft.

'Many hopeful pilots did not make the grade, and those who did possessed great stamina and a high morale, so when they flew a glider into battle they possessed great confidence in their ability.

They also had respect for the RAF pilots and crews of the planes towing them. When I piloted my glider to Normandy on D-Day the weather was not good and it was very dark. The sky was cloudy, and when I released from the Halifax towing me, at 0300 hours, I could not see the ground. We had been briefed that the Germans had planted upright poles in the ground over a large area to counter any glider attack, and paratroops had gone in ahead of us to blow the poles up. Many of them were destroyed but there were a lot left, and many gliders collided with them. In the event, I landed in an area that was free of obstruction, but when we came to unload a bulldozer it was stuck. I hailed the driver of a passing jeep and together we secured a long rope to the bulldozer and hauled it free and I sent it on its way to clear areas for landing strips. Just before take-off a paratrooper had hitched a lift in my glider because he was anxious not to miss the action. After we landed he disappeared into the night. He was a man of few words; I often wondered what happened to him.'

Amongst the many glider pilots who participated in the D-Day invasion many were killed in action or seriously wounded. Molly Prescott, who was then a young nurse at RAF Wroughton Hospital remembers casualties being brought in from Normandy, still in their blood-stained uniforms, many of them receiving blood transfusions and saline drips. She particularly remembers one young glider pilot who had been badly burned. 'Both his arms and hands were heavily bandaged and, because he could do nothing for himself, I used to give him drinks, feed him and minister to his needs. I never heard him complain and I felt very humble when I thought of glider pilots flying troops and equipment in flimsy aircraft, to be released over enemy-held territory and left to glide down to uncertain landings, and in some cases to die inside their gliders whilst still in the air.'

Mary Bell, a nursing sister at Walton Hospital, Liverpool, joined the Queen Alexandra Imperial Nursing Service early in the war and she went to Normandy three days after D-Day. 'Among the first wounded men to come into my care was a young glider pilot, little more than a boy. He was gravely ill and as I tended him he asked for a cigarette. I did not have one and it wrung my heart to deny his wish, so I sent an orderly to get some cigarettes. Unfortunately, before he returned, the young pilot died.'

A Horsa Mk. II.

A Hamilcar in tow. Hamilcars were big and heavy and could carry large pay-loads. Typical loads were Tetrarch tanks and crews, plus ammunition, 17 pounder guns, trailers and men; 3-ton lorries; heavy high explosive ammunition; excavators; heavy machinery; bridge sections; etc.

16

Operation Dingson

6 June 1944

On the night of D-Day ten gliders took off at 2200 hours, to fly to St Helène, a few miles south of Lorient, a port in Britanny. The gliders carried French SAS troops, jeeps, weapons and ammunition. In failing light they approached their landing zone, which was illuminated by the flames of a burning house. Nine gliders landed safely, the tenth crashed among trees and the occupants were given shelter by Maquis, who also tended their injuries. The other pilots and their French passengers, together with the jeeps, weapons and ammunition, were taken to the Maquis headquarters, some distance away. It was an isolated farm and all the Maquis there wore Resistance Movement armbands and were well armed. When fighting they gave no quarter and expected none, and there were always some absent, usually travelling in jeeps with machine-guns mounted fore and aft. None of them had any regard for danger when they sabotaged, killed, or took prisoners.

The glider pilots saw only a little action as the Maquis did not trust their limited French, and Captain Clarke, the senior glider pilot, was charged with keeping them from wandering off.

Prisoners were housed in a very large pigsty that was still in use by the pigs, and the glider pilots were detailed to guard them. Life at the farm was raw and hard, with limited sanitary arrangements in the open, in an old unworked quarry.

Later, the pilots learned that American tanks were approaching and the Maquis drove them into the town, in a lorry, just as the leading tanks arrived. None of the glider pilots were in uniform as they had left England dressed as civilians, with nothing to identify them with the army. However, Captain Clarke eventually convinced the Americans of their true identities and they were later taken to Vannes, from where they were transported to Rennes.

There the pilots were interviewed by intelligence officers, who gave them money and cigarettes. A few days later the pilots were taken to an aerodrome used by the Allies at Rennes, and 11 days after their departure from England they were flown back to Netheravon, their unusual operation completed.

Three weeks after D-Day Ronald Hobbs, DFC and bar, who was a squadron leader, was detailed to fly his Halifax IX to France to collect a Hamilcar glider. His brief was to fly with minimum crew and equipment to reduce the plane's overall weight as much as possible.

Recalling the trip, Ronald said, 'We took off from Tarrant Rushton, crossed the English Channel and located the Hamilcar, which was standing at the end of a field that extended some nine hundred yards. There was an orchard at the far end. The Halifax had only three of its six fuel tanks in use and I landed the aircraft in "fighter" style before taxiing up to the Hamilcar and hitching up. I could not switch off the Halifax's engines as it was without starting gear, so we created a great deal of dust. I sent a member of my crew over to the Hamilcar pilot, a captain I recall, with a request that as soon as possible during take-off he took the glider into the high-position to "nurse" my fuel. He signified his assent and soon afterwards, on full throttle, we took off, just scraping over the apple trees in the orchard, to begin our flight back to Tarrant Rushton, where we landed one and a half hours later.

‘I had assumed that we had towed back an empty Hamilcar but when the huge glider sank onto its flat underside and the hinged nose opened, two beautiful-looking racehorses were led out!

Had I realised what the cargo was when we hitched up in the French field I would have thought twice about that take-off. However, all’s well that ends well and I wonder what became of those racehorses and whether they sired any winners.’

17

South of France

Operation Anvil-Dragoon, August 1944

The Independent Squadron left Italy at Putignano and travelled to Oudjda, French Morocco, where it established itself and engaged in training and ferrying new Waco gliders from Casablanca to Oudjda.

Oudjda was an American Airborne Forces Training Centre, and the station was home to a mixture of service personnel, Americans, British, French and South Africans, an Allied conglomerate that got on very well together. Then, after American Thanksgiving Day, the Independent Squadron was ordered back to Sicily, the first gliders leaving Oudjda just before Christmas 1943, and the squadron set up its headquarters at Camiso. The movement of the squadron was completed in a week.

Camiso had been badly damaged by bombing during the Sicily invasion, but the squadron's personnel soon transformed damaged buildings into comfortable billets, and also enjoyed some very good flying, with American C47s employed as tug planes. A variety of flights took place over a period of five months and the squadrons flying skill, by day and night, was increased.

During the time the squadron was at Camiso it was joined by a pathfinder unit of the 22nd Parachute Brigade with whom the

Allied airborne landings in Southern France. British gliders and towing aircraft lined up at an Italian airfield before taking off, 1944.

Independent Squadron was to operate in the South of France. The paras and the glider pilots enjoyed a good rapport and worked together in training. The pathfinder paras were to precede the gliders into the South of France and lay out the landing zones.

Shortly before the planned invasion date the American Wacos were found to be unable to carry the British 6-pounder anti-tank guns and their towing vehicles, The Independent Squadron was therefore re-equipped with the larger Horsas, which could lift greater loads. The Horsas were taken to Sicily from various locations, together with maintenance teams.

Training then continued with the Horsas, and in June 1944 the squadron moved to Guido, Italy, and a month later north to Tarquinia on Italy's west coast. In early August the glider pilots and the crews of the C47 tug planes were briefed. The objective was to be the South of France, in the area of Le Muy, north of Fréjus, which is south-west of Cannes.

Breakfast on 15 August 1944 was served at 0400 hours and a half-hour later the aircrews were assembling at their aircraft. At 0530 hours the first combination moved off and within a half-hour all combinations were flying over the Mediterranean. However, after only an hour's flying the formation turned back to Tarquinia because the landing zone was obscured by mist.

At 1400 hours the tug-glider combinations were again airborne and after flying for four hours over the sea, the force of British and American gliders crossed the southern French coast and went on towards their landing zones 10 miles inland. They landed over 2,500 men, more than 200 guns, 220 vehicles and 500 tons of equipment. The leading glider was piloted by Major R. Coulthard, a very experienced pilot, but he was badly injured when, landing among upright anti-invasion poles in a vineyard, his Horsa struck one of them. However, none of the men he carried were injured and his cargo of guns was undamaged. The Horsa was quickly unloaded and the men and their guns were almost immediately in action.

The task force had achieved its aim of landing troops, arms, vehicles and equipment behind the enemy coast defences, so cutting off German reinforcements from the north. Operation Anvil-Dragoon was a complete success.

18

Arnhem

Operation Market Garden, 17 September 1944

Following upon the occupation of Paris by the Allies (25 August) their forces went into Belgium to liberate Brussels (3 September). Then however, a strategic dissension began to divide the Allied High Command and it was to have its effect on the planning and outcome of the Arnhem operation.

Following upon the invasion of the south of France there were three Allied army groups in north-west Europe, two American and one British. General Eisenhower favoured a 'broad front' strategy, attacking the Germans on all fronts, from Switzerland to the North Sea, simultaneously. General Montgomery, though, preferred a 'narrow front' concept, giving maximum priority of supplies, air cover and reinforcements to his 21st Group in Holland for a thrust through the Netherlands to the Ruhr, where the consequent loss of Germany's heavy industries would lead to the end of the war.

Predictably, the Americans objected to Monty's plan, one of the most outspoken objectors being General Patton, who did not wish to be a spectator while Britain won the war. Eisenhower eventually gave way to British pressure and General Montgomery was given the use of American forces and priority over supplies.

The plan for 'Market Garden' envisaged two separate phases. 'Market' to be the creation of a corridor by the American 101

Airborne Division, from Eindhoven–Grave, and the 82 Airborne Division to establish its central section at Grave–Nijmegen, with bridges over two canals north of Eindhoven secured, and two other bridges secured over the Rivers Maas and Waal. Simultaneously, the British 1st Airborne Division were to capture and hold the bridge crossing the Rhine at Arnhem, Holland, for 48 hours, until the arrival of reinforcements.

The British 30 Corps, led by the Guards Armoured Division, under Operation Garden, were to link up with them along the single road through Oosterbeek, before reaching Arnhem bridge and going on into the Ruhr area of Germany. The commander of 30 Corps was Lieutenant General Sir Brian Horrocks and of the British 1st Airborne Division Major General Roy E. Urquhart. In the event there were, unfortunately, too few aircraft available to drop all the required Americans, and only the British 1st Parachute Brigade and a part of The Glider Pilot Regiment were consequently able to participate on Day 1. The remainder were to follow on later.

The plan's most important feature was that those glider pilots taking part would largely have to remain in the landing area in a defensive role pending the arrival of the next day's second phase. That effectively reduced the combatant strength available at the bridge. Inadequate intelligence reports from the area had left the Allies unaware that both the German 9th and 10th SS Panzer Divisions were resting near Arnhem, and it had been falsely reported that the enemy anti-aircraft defences around Arnhem were very strong. It was decided therefore that glider landings and parachute drops should be well away from the city and thus well away from the guns. The decision was also encouraged by the fact that the land around Oosterbeek was well wooded and would give protection initially. It was, however, about 8 miles north-west of Arnhem.

The total number of glider pilots to take part was 1,126. Drawbacks of the plan proved to be twofold: the rendezvous for the troops after landing was some 2 miles from the area in which the gliders were to land and, in the event, the greater proportion of glider pilots on the first day were committed to action instead of remaining to defend the landing zone.

The glider-borne operation began at 0900 hours on Sunday, 17 September 1944 and at the outset achieved complete surprise, the men being welcomed by joyful Oosterbeek villagers. The Germans had been caught off guard and were surprised at the timing and size of the operation, but German troops stationed nearby were quickly organized into taking counter-measures, and the distance that the British had to travel to reach the bridge at Arnhem gave the enemy ample time to prepare for their arrival.

On the first day 350 gliders were in operation, one of them piloted by Colonel Chatterton, with Major General 'Boy' Browning, his jeep and his staff aboard. It was during that flight that Browning uttered the words that led to the post-war film title *A Bridge Too Far*. What he said to Chatterton was, 'The troops are being asked to do a lot, the bridge is likely to be too far distant from the landing zone.'

'Dickie' Bird was briefed to fly with the second lift on 18 September. 'Almost everyone not flying on the first day,' he said, 'watched the departure of the first wave on the Sunday. We wished them good luck, many of the WAAFs and NAAFI girls were looking on anxiously and we awaited the return of the tug planes, counting them as they returned to check whether all had got back.'

The night before the operation everyone was confined to camp and spent the hours in different ways, some at the bar, others writing letters, playing cards, or just thinking. John Hemmings recalls; 'I and my second pilot, Alan Boon, spent a long time studying a map of our landing zone and the route to Arnhem. Alan Boon, before the war, was a member of the Sadler's Wells Ballet Company and had joined the Royal Corps of Signals before transferring to The Glider Pilot Regiment. I had been an AOP pilot before training as a glider pilot and it was the first glider operation for both of us.'

Syd Dodd considered himself to be a father figure to the young glider pilots as he had joined the Royal Artillery in 1935 when most glider pilots were still at school. He went to France early in the war and had experienced the trauma of Dunkirk. He joined The Glider Pilot Regiment in 1942. Majors Hugh Bartlett and Billy Griffiths, inseparable friends, had both been county cricketers. After the war Bartlett captained Sussex and Griffiths played for England. Another pilot, Stan Holden, had played soccer for Fulham F C.

Syd Dodd and his co-pilot Harry Parkinson had a good flight to Holland on Day 1 and landed north-west of Oosterbeek with the 30 men of the Border Regiment he had flown to Holland, and made off quickly to the rendezvous at a corner of a wood. There Dodd and Parkinson boarded a jeep that set off for Arnhem, with tracer bullets occasionally flying. Their mission was to do a recce and report what was happening there. Returning, he was sent to Divisional Headquarters at the Hartenstein Hotel, Oosterbeek, where he later dug-in on the lawn in front of the building as shelling had begun. The next day, because of his earlier artillery experience, he was assigned to a 6-pounder anti-tank gun.

Later, with other pilots, Syd went along the river road towards Arnhem, but found that the enemy had occupied buildings around the bridge. They took up positions along the side of a field, with Germans in position on the other side and shots were intermittently exchanged. The position of the men was getting desperate as the days passed and Dodd had several times fired a PIAT (projectile infantry anti-tank) at German half-tracks, but morale was getting low. One day some American Dakotas flew over to drop supplies but all but one bale fell into the area occupied by the Germans. The odd bale fell closer to the British lads and Syd Dodd, at some risk, retrieved it, only to find when it was opened, that the bale contained battle-dress and red berets!

The only officer the British lads had with them was Captain

Pickwood and he continually rallied the men, but the real problem was the lack of information. Dodd was amazed that men could go so long without sleep. Food too was short but someone found a lot of tomatoes. The weekend brought no respite from the Germans' weapons but the enemy had gradually extended their position along the other two sides of the field. On the second Sunday Dodd was wounded in the back and thigh by a mortar shell and rain was slanting down. Soon afterwards the small airborne force was overrun by the Germans and taken prisoner.

Alan Boon and I had landed a platoon of the South Staffordshire Regiment and in Oosterbeek we met up with Major Robert Cain of that regiment, but he got a lift in a jeep going to Arnhem. There was no room for us, so with others we went on foot towards our objective. At Den Brink crossroads we saw an abandoned bullet-ridden German staff car. On the outskirts of Arnhem our group suddenly came under fire from snipers' bullets and mortars, which were very accurate and caused casualties as well as halting our progress. We took what cover we could and were pinned down for a long time, with any slight movement attracting a sniper's bullet. Crouching in what seemed to be inadequate cover, I felt that nothing could prevent the unseen enemy from gradually picking us off. Was this the way that men facing execution felt?

At last, in a brief interlude of calm, we began to inch forward and soon got caught up in street fighting. My earlier feeling of inevitability changed, the adrenalin rose and our advance moved on purposely. Such fighting caused considerable expenditure of ammunition, and men replenished from the ammunition pouches of dead men. Firing from one particular building was claiming casualties, so, with the remaining members of the group with whom I was travelling, we stormed the building, gaining entry via some ground-floor windows. After having quietened all opposition inside the building, we moved on towards the bridge from building to building but progress was slow. I had acquired a Sten gun from a fallen soldier. These mass-produced guns were effective automatics and I was very glad to have one.

Exposed to enemy automatic and sniper's fire, glider pilots, airborne infantrymen and paratroopers moved forward slowly, whenever there was a lull in the hail of bullets. Many were killed and wounded as they fought their way towards Arnhem bridge. Inside a house a small group of them had taken up firing positions before moving off to another house. General Roy Urquhart and Brigadier Lathbury appeared to have gone missing; they had not been seen for some time and it was thought that they might have been taken prisoner. In fact they were holed up in a house for a couple of days, unable to get out. Then, as Staff Sergeant 'Will' Willerby looked from a window in another house, he was surprised to see a smoke-bomb land in a back garden and under its cover two men running towards the garden wall. The first man got over but the second missed his footing and slipped back. 'I recognised him as the general,' said Will, 'and as he gathered himself for a second attempt Captain Hemmings appeared and putting both hands under the general's backside, heaved him up and over. Seeing me, he grinned and said, "If I get back I'll be able to dine out on that one". We all heard later that the general and the brigadier eventually linked up with the HQ staff.'

A South Staffordshire man was shot through the head and while John Hemmings and others were in the ground-floor room of a three-storey house a grenade came through the window, dropped onto the floor and rolled across the carpet. It did not explode and quick as a flash Boon pounced on it and in one fluid movement picked it up and hurled it back through the window and it exploded outside almost immediately. Soon afterwards they all left the house by a back door and began to cross the garden, intending to go over a wall into another garden. It was then that a shell hit the house behind them and a piece of shrapnel hit the author's arm.

Gordon Jenks, a Hamilcar pilot, awoke before reveille on Sunday, 17 September, with a mild hangover from a convivial night before. Unable to eat any breakfast he went straight to the truck that was to take him to the Halifax–Hamilcar combination, which stood adjacent to Halifax–Horsa combinations, all ready for take-

A General Aircraft Hamilcar.

off. Jenks, a very experienced pilot, was soon inside his huge Hamilcar glider checking the controls and intercom, then looking over the load his glider was to carry to a spot some 60 miles behind German lines. The load consisted of a 17-pounder anti-tank gun and its trailer, a lorry and high explosive shells. Also travelling were eight men.

In the air during the flight he saw Hamilcars, Horsas and their tug planes, looking like a solid mass in the sky. As the combinations approached the landing zones German anti-aircraft batteries opened fire, but rocket-firing Typhoons escorting the combinations dived down, firing at the gun sites.

Jenks' Hamilcar was hit by shrapnel which put both the air-speed indicator and the altimeter out of action. All around him were gliders going down towards the ground, and as he prepared to land, Jenks saw another Hamilcar going too fast and too low, hit the railway embankment, somersault and burst into flames. Another one landed fast on soft ground, dug its wheels in and turned over onto its back. Jenks got down safely.

Soon after crossing the Dutch coast, carrying a platoon of the Border Regiment and a handcart of mortar bombs, plus mortars, Lieutenant John Place looked down at the flooded area below, then asked his co-pilot, Ralph Maltby, to take the controls while he studied a map. Only minutes afterwards there was a bang in the cockpit and Ralph Maltby slumped in his seat – dead! It was an alarming experience for Place, who realised as he grabbed the controls that if he too were to be killed, no one else could fly the Horsa and land it!

Sergeant Arthur Rigby, soon after landing in the Horsa of which he was one of the pilots, climbed aboard the last truck in a column of vehicles travelling towards Arnhem. The column reached the city and as it was getting dusk, it halted in the shade of some trees. Later they moved onto a road running alongside the river. Rigby and others then dismounted and went with glider pilots Captains Cole and Simpson into a small park, close to the bridge, where fighting was in progress. Rigby could identify automatic weapons and rifle fire.

Colonel John Frost and the 2nd Parachute Battalion had established themselves at the northern end of the bridge, with German troops advancing to hold the southern end. By the next morning Frost's men had been reduced in number and they were fighting for their lives. The South Staffordshire's and some glider pilots arrived to give their support and in the darkness of the second night Arnhem looked like a vision of hell, with shells, mortars and automatic fire finding their marks, and buildings on fire. The people of Arnhem were in their cellars or air-raid shelters, and in a house illuminated by candles, with broken windows and the walls pitted by shrapnel, Rigby and others had moved pieces of furniture to screen windows where some men had taken up firing positions while their comrades took some rest.

Major Robert Cain, a tough rugby player with a jutting chin, frequently exposed himself to danger as, from the south end of Arnhem Bridge, the Germans stepped up their attack with artillery, mortars and tanks. On a number of occasions he went forward to hurl grenades, firing a Bren from the hip. Meanwhile colonel John Frost and his diminishing force continued to keep the Germans at bay.

Glider pilots Captain Cole and Staff Sergeant Gault had been killed and Lieutenant Bird wounded. When a German tank advanced across the bridge Cain appeared from cover and got down full-length on the bridge and aimed a PIAT. The tank was too close for its gunners to depress their guns low enough to hit him and Cain scored a direct hit that blew the tank up in spectacular fashion.

In one of the streets the Germans had cornered a number of officers and men, all of whom were wounded or out of ammunition. Word was passed among them that many glider pilots had been wounded, killed, or were missing. Among them were Roger Craft, Tim Matthews, Jim Bonham, Denis Cartlidge,

Eric Phillips and Jim Curley.

General Urquhart's whereabouts were unknown but rumour had it that he was a prisoner. In fact he had been captured but later escaped and rejoined the British Airborne men.

Flying Officer Wallace piloted an Albemarle towing a Horsa, the pilots of which were Staff Sergeants Woodcock and Wilson. The Horsa was heavily loaded, with a jeep, anti-tank gun and trailer, plus the gun crew and ammunition. The flight was made at low level because of the heavy load, and the Albemarle was not very manoeuvrable. 'I felt like a goldfish in a bowl, wondering where the cat was,' said Wally. 'At the point of release tug planes and gliders were turning in all directions, trying to avoid trouble as tracers came up. I did not envy the tasks of the glider pilots either going in to land or on the ground afterwards. I did not see either Woodcock or Wilson again, and do not know whether they were killed or captured.' Wally Wallace now lives in New Zealand.

On the western side of Oosterbeek, divisional headquarters had been set up at the Hartenstein Hotel, a splendid building set among lawns and screened by flowering shrubs. Soon, with the divisional flag flying, glider pilots, including Victor Wade, were digging slit trenches in the lawns.

Lieutenant Turrel and his second pilot were shot up and forced to land away from the LZ but were helped by local Dutchmen, who led the pilots and their passengers north, and after a few skirmishes with the enemy they reached the Hartenstein Hotel.

Born in Canada, Robert Garnett came with his parents to England when he was nine. After leaving school he joined The King's Shropshire Light Infantry and was commissioned in 1941. Two years later he volunteered for The Glider Pilot Regiment because, in his teens, he had been an enthusiastic member of a gliding club.

Posted to 'E' Squadron, No. 2 Wing, like so many other glider

A.W.E. Spijkers
NED. HERV. KERK
OOSTERBEEK

pilots he suffered the frustrations of standing-to for operations, and then finding that they had been cancelled as, with his fellow pilots and troops aboard, he sat tense and poised to go on the runway. Garnett's initiation, when it came during 'Market Garden', was a baptism of fire. Having landed his glider, against a hail of German shells and bullets, he and the platoon with him fought for 48 hours without sleep. They managed to break out and again met strong opposition on the far side of Oosterbeek. The sky was full of coloured tracers, orange and mauve, and the firing was heavy. Lieutenant Garnett and a sergeant went forward, while the rest gave covering fire from a house, but the garden fences and hedges slowed down progress somewhat, and eventually, being unable to find anywhere to break out, Garnett and the NCO returned to the house to rejoin the others. The enemy pressed closer and tanks appeared, adding fire and Garnett and company withdrew from the back and took cover in a small wood. They continued to resist the enemy until 25 September, when they were overrun and Garnett and the survivors of his group were taken prisoner. He was repatriated in April 1945 and continued with The Glider Pilot Regiment until 1950.

Descriptive of the fighting in Arnhem is the following story from Sergeant Archie Simms. 'When we reached the town outskirts it was like a normal Sunday. Someone waved from the window of a house and wished us good luck. Then we came across odd machine-gun emplacements from which we came under fire, but we were not held up. At one point there was a damaged machine-gun with two dead gunners sprawled over it. About two hundred metres from the bridge I saw two glider pilot officers, Captain Hemmings and Captain Simpson, they were both firing automatics. Then they joined us and the former told us to go into a house and barricade it and he gave us fire orders. A German tank approached and someone, I couldn't see from where, fired a PIAT and the tank seemed to lift off the road in slow motion before blowing up.

'On the third morning I saw two glider pilots, Lieutenant Tayler and Staff Sergeant Mitchell, go into a house across the road. They had two infantrymen with them. The lieutenant was killed during the battle but "Mitch" survived and after the war went to Africa to work on a ground-nuts project.

'During the night two or three of us left the house we were in and reached the bridge, where Colonel Frost and Major Cain were performing great deeds. In fact the major was later awarded the Victoria Cross. An officer of the South Staffs sent some men with a flame-thrower to attack a German pillbox and the result of the attack was horrific.'

There were lorries on fire along the river and John Frost's men had suffered casualties. The worst wounded had been evacuated into buildings. The next day saw the Germans mount an attack with 40-mm guns and the number of burning buildings increased. Timbers that no longer burnt fiercely still smouldered. Frost's men were managing to keep the Germans at bay with some artillery help and mortars.

Danny Prewett remembers, 'Our Forty-eight hours emergency rations had been eked out until early on Day Four but by then we had only some potatoes and grapes that someone had found. We had no water and an officer suggested that some of us should try to get back to Oosterbeek to try to open up an escape route. Those who drew the short straws were the ones to make the attempt, which they all knew had risks as it meant going through, or around, enemy positions. For myself, I remained, was taken prisoner, escaped within an hour, but was recaptured and ended my war in a prison in Germany.'

Captain Simpson had assigned Sergeant Rigby and others to a nearby house on the corner of two streets. It proved to be expensively furnished, with beautiful cut glass and pictures. The men positioned themselves at the windows, using some very expensive-looking furniture as screens. In one upper room Rigby found a fragile old lady in bed, too weak to have gone with those of her family who had left. A Tiger tank advancing along the street fired a number of shells and one went right through a wall, filling a room with rubble and dust. It did not explode so one of the men carried it outside and deposited it in the garden. During the time they were there, the house was hit several times and the bedridden lady was killed by a piece of shrapnel in the neck as she lay in her bed.

Eventually the men left the house, exiting from ground-floor windows at the back. A few days later the house was set alight by incendiary bombs and burnt fiercely, providing a funeral pyre for the old Dutch lady. By that time, Rigby and some others were in another house. They were hungry and thirsty but spent a quiet night free of any disturbance. The three glider pilots in the small group had got hold of a PIAT and with its only two bombs awaited another attack. It came at dawn with the Germans setting up an attack with infantry and 88-mm mobile guns. It was a determined effort that became quite hectic as the enemy used everything in an attempt to dislodge the small force. Then, suddenly the attack stopped, only occasional mortar bombs were falling in the area, and although they had suffered casualties the little airborne force felt their spirits lift.

Nearby a house was ablaze and two glider pilots, Staff Sergeant White and Sergeant Winkworth, were killed and a number of others were wounded. One of them, Charlie Watts, had his arm severed at the elbow and he stood dazedly looking at the bloody stump.

At the bridge Lieutenant Colonel Frost's mind went back to the planning stage of the operation. His 2nd Parachute Battalion had been ordered to capture three bridges in the Arnhem area: one the river bridge at Arnhem that he was now defending, the railway bridge outside of the town and a bridge over the main road. He had believed from the first that capturing three bridges from such distant dropping zones was asking too much of the paratroops and glider-borne troops. At the same time he had been optimistic that his men would succeed because intelligence passed to the Allies had said that the Germans were thin on the ground and low in morale.

That belief, at first, was bolstered by the lack of enemy troops on the first day and the welcome from the people of Oosterbeek. People in their gardens, walking in the street and working in the fields called out, 'Thank you for coming.' They had offered drinks, fruit and flowers, mainly orange-coloured marigolds. Then, unexpectedly, shooting began. The civilian women and children screamed and scattered and a British soldier fell dead. But still Frost hoped that by the time the vanguard reached Arnhem Bridge the rest of the Parachute Brigade would not be far away. Frost's men continued to advance, with glider-borne troops and some glider pilots with them. There were skirmishes en route but Frost's men pushed on, leaving German casualties behind them. At a crossroads there was a hot engagement but the British reached Arnhem, regrouped near the river, then took up position at the northern end of the bridge.

Two glider pilots had salvaged a Bren carrier from a crashed Hamilcar and then joined some Staffords. The Germans had surprisingly found a complete set of 'Market Garden' operation plans in a crashed US Waco at Nijmegen, and had marshalled their troops to halt the British. Civilians had gone into their basements, or had taken themselves off to other areas. Despite this the British felt confident that 30 Corps would arrive to relieve them quite soon.

A company of paratroops moving to capture the railway bridge had it blown up in their faces. One disadvantage the men could not overcome was that they had been trained to land behind and close to the enemy and not to have to cover 7 or 8 miles on foot, crossing obstacles in the face of determined opposition.

Once the paratroops, South Staffs and glider pilots reached the river bridge it was almost dark and the men occupied buildings dominating the north end and its approaches.

Now Frost and his men had got to the northern end of the bridge and were in buildings scattered around, facing great odds. He had sent a platoon to cross the bridge, a dangerous mission as they were met by intense fire, The survivors, deciding that a direct approach was impossible, 'mouseholed' their way through a series of buildings by blasting holes in the party walls. Then Germans arrived in vehicles, but some among the British platoon set the vehicles alight and the glare from the flames and the intense heat prevented any other approach until morning.

Frost had also despatched an officer to recce, to ascertain what other British troops were in the area, and to determine if there was any other way of getting across the river. The officer returned with negative answers. The following morning a column of German panzer armoured cars appeared but were routed, and a number were destroyed by British anti-tank guns.

Fighting continued through successive days and nights, while casualties mounted on both sides. The British were running short of ammunition; when engaged in close-quarter fighting ammunition is vital, so the colonel's instructions were to conserve ammunition by firing only when certain of making a kill.

Food and water shortage was another of Frost's problems because not only had he and his men to be fed, but so had the many German prisoners they had taken. The Germans had increased their artillery assault, using 150-mm guns that fired 100-pound shells. Fortunately, British mortars scored a direct hit on the ammunition stacked by one gun, killing its crew and disabling the gun in the explosion.

'All day the Germans pounded us,' said Frost, 'and I was concerned about our wounded. Water had run out and many of the wounded needed to be evacuated. During one day the Germans sent a message, under a flag of truce, asking me to meet their commander to discuss surrender terms. I refused.'

That evening German tanks appeared in the half-light, swinging their guns right and left, inflicting damage and filling the air with the dust of falling masonry and acrid smoke. The padre was kept busy tending the wounded, comforting the dying and praying for those already dead. Some of the men brought up a 6-pounder gun and quietened the enemy. All the men were very tired and still 30 Corps had not reached the area. Colonel Frost was wounded in both legs but was determined that his second-in-command and other officers should hold their ground and resist all enemy attacks.

Glider pilot Bill Nixon spent the night in a slit trench he and others had dug close to the bridge. Soon after dawn broke they heard staff Sergeant Ainsworth, who was in an adjacent slit trench with his second pilot, Sergeant Rigby, call out that it was his birthday. Someone answered, 'You should be so lucky!' While another, without thinking called, 'If you don't cop it, you'll probably have a happier one next year.'

'I had a quick whip-round among those with me and then eased myself out of cover and crawled over to where Ainsworth was and gave him a few boiled sweets and a piece of chocolate as a birthday present.'

The scene at the north end of the bridge, described by Sergeant Major 'Peddler' Palmer, was of raging fires over a wide area, with 'fireworks' displays of tracers and exploding ammunition. Buildings and lorries were ablaze and one German lorry carrying ammunition had been blown up. Glider pilots answered a call to assemble in a municipal building, where they were detailed for various duties. Among them were Rigby and Ainsworth, who went to a nearby house. Ainsworth has said, 'We came under fire from a sniper who was behind a chimney stack on a nearby roof. Arthur Rigby and myself conferred, then I fired a couple of shots at the corner of the stack. They must have been close to the sniper as he moved slightly and partially exposed himself. As he did, Rigby, fired some rapid shots with a Bren as another sniper fired a shot at Rigby, but he missed, the bullet embedding itself in the window frame.'

The battle had become a war of attrition, with a regular pattern of bombardment followed by attempted advances by infantry and armoured vehicles. The men of the airborne forces were almost at the end of their tether. Among the airborne soldiers captured on Tuesday, 19 September, were two privates of the 1st Parachute Battalion who later escaped by jumping from the lorry carrying them. They set out towards Oosterbeek and on the way joined some men of the 3rd Battalion. The following afternoon they reached the outskirts of Oosterbeek but were then held up by a German force between them and their goal. With glider pilot Sergeant Wyatt, one of the escapees, Private Charlton, got into a house, and joined Lieutenant Curtis, Sergeant Callaghan and Private Cole. Douglas Charlton had a PIAT but when a German Tiger tank advanced towards the house the weapon misfired and the tank blasted the house. The only casualty was Lieutenant Curtis, whose right leg was blown off.

The survivors fought on until the withdrawal on 26 September. Fighting in Oosterbeek was fierce, with many examples of bravery. Glider pilot Lieutenant (as he was then,) Mike Dauncey in particular showed great gallantry. For five days he took command of a party of men defending the guns of the Air Landing Light Regiment, Royal Artillery, under continual attack by tanks and infantry. Dauncey led several attacks with great determination, regaining lost positions, ignoring automatic and small-arms fire despite being wounded three times. On 24 September he lost the sight of one eye but continued to lead his men, inflicting heavy losses on the enemy. On 25 September his position was attacked by a self-propelled gun. Mike Dauncey, single-handed, attacked the self-propelled gun with gammon bombs and was again wounded, then taken prisoner by the Germans. For his courage and devotion to duty Lieutenant Dauncey was awarded the Distinguished Service Order. In December 1944 he escaped from a prison hospital and made his way back to British lines.

From the upper floor of a three-storey house glider pilots Ainsworth and Rigby watched as two medical orderlies with a stretcher ran across the street to a wounded man lying on the opposite pavement. Just as they lifted the man onto a stretcher a sniper killed all three. The two glider pilots felt sickened.

The author recalls, 'Many houses were on fire and the flames illuminated the area. There were many acts of bravery among the airborne men as they fought continuously through days and nights, and looking at some of those near me I scarcely recognised them. Their faces were grimy and drawn, their eyes tired from the lack of sleep that would have given them respite from pain and the horrors of war; very tired men, who were not flag-waving patriots but were fighting for what they hoped would become a better world. Men who had seen comrades die and who were near the point of exhaustion. Men with haunted faces and whose urgent youth had slipped away from them.

'Bullets ricocheted from the walls of buildings and mortars and shells caused humps of masonry and brickwork to fly in all directions. Glass and debris lay everywhere, parked German vehicles were on fire and the noise was deafening. In a house, finding the taps dry, a corporal baled water from the lavatory cistern with which to brew tea while comrades engaged the enemy.

'Some Polish paratroopers had dropped on the fifth day and were very frustrated at being unable to reach the bridge. One of their officers, Captain Zwolanski, went off to look for a place where he could swim the river to attempt to rally support. Supplies of ammunition were very low and a group of us decided to try to get back into Oosterbeek and to rejoin the forces there. Three groups of six men each, led by myself, Lieutenant Perkins and Sergeant Braithwaite, set off separately and, eventually, after a number of engagements, the three groups all reached the perimeter of Oosterbeek, although with their numbers reduced.'

One of the glider pilots to land on Day 1, Colin McHaven, had a girlfriend in England of whom he was very fond. Very close to each other, they both thought of marriage but McHaven said they should wait until after the war as he had a premonition that he might die. He was killed on Tuesday, 19 September.

Examples of the courage so often displayed by glider pilots, paratroops, infantrymen and others, also came from the padres, doctors and medical orderlies, all of whom were extremely brave and selfless. One padre acted as a loader to an anti-tank gun when a German Tiger tank began firing indiscriminately at houses occupied by Dutch families.

When bad weather prevented the 1st Polish Parachute Brigade from going to Arnhem on Tuesday, 19 September, the Poles were an unhappy lot. However, they finally took off on the 21st. When they arrived over the dropping zone, shells were exploding around them, and as they dropped enemy tracer burst among them. Captain Lee Matecheck dropped and landed separated from his Polish comrades but linked up with three glider pilots, Sergeants Nixon, Whyke and Walters. They tried to get to Arnhem but found themselves under heavy fire from an enemy determined to stop them. Then a German self-propelled gun appeared and the four men went into one of a pair of houses shell-shattered and deserted by their Dutch owners. Gradually the enemy encroached on the house, keeping the four men well occupied. Matecheck had acquired a Bren gun, which he used effectively. The next morning Whyke was killed and Nixon wounded, and during the night the survivors got away in the dark and found a new position, which they shared with glider pilot Victor Wade.

Stanley Pearson made a good landing at Arnhem and remained until the next day in the landing area. Afterwards he set off with others towards Arnhem Bridge but got stuck in the perimeter until the final day.

During the afternoon of that fateful day, together with fellow veterans of the River Orne–Caen Canal *coup de main*, Jim Wallwork, Oliver Boland, Len Guthrie and Stanley Pearson helped to stretch parachute cords from tree to tree to guide the troops withdrawing after dark.

Lieutenant Colonel Pat Glover recalled going into a house with a few of his paras and, after making sure that there were no enemy inside, detailing the men to take up firing positions upstairs. 'Soon afterwards I was joined by three glider pilots, Captain Hemmings and two NCOs, Stevenson and Allen, together with a Polish sergeant. Not long afterwards the Germans attempted an infantry attack from the rear and, as they closed in, my men upstairs opened fire. Meanwhile the three glider pilots, the Pole and myself took up positions on the ground floor. The Germans were forced to take cover but lobbed grenades over, most of them falling short. Eventually they withdrew, leaving behind some dead. Two Germans helped a wounded comrade over a wall and we left them to it; there seemed no point in cold-blooded murder. During the night a party of Germans attempted another attack but were again driven off. By daybreak we were all pretty tired and I organised a rest rota among my men, while Captain Hemmings told his men to get some sleep. The Polish sergeant had left during the night to try to locate his compatriots.

'We were hemmed in, and the long hoped-for arrival of British troops to assist us was not forthcoming. A patrol of four paras and an officer appeared further down the street, but they came under machine-gun fire and were cut down. Thirsty, I explored the house for water but the taps were dry and the lavatory cistern empty. From the reflected glow in the windows across the street I knew that an adjoining house was on fire and it was not long before we could smell the smoke. During late morning we took the opportunity to leave from the back of the house. The smoke from the nearby fire had aggravated our thirsts and our eyes were red-rimmed and smarting. We separated into small groups seeking our own salvation.'

In Arnhem, Lieutenant Colonel Frost and his surviving officers and men had been taken prisoner after finally being overrun. The brigade staff had been operating as snipers and the initial exhilaration of the flight out of England, their welcome by the Dutch people, and the adrenalin-fired journey overland to Arnhem, with the expectation of support from 30 Corps, had deteriorated into a weariness brought about by continuous fighting, no reserves, lack of food and thirst. John Frost, wounded, had been given morphia and Major Gough had assumed command. Although determined to hold out at the northern end of the bridge, they were eventually sealed off by increasing numbers of Germans, who encircled them and then moved inwards from all sides. Brigade Headquarters had caught fire and there was no water with which to fight the flames. Added to this the brigade doctor feared for the safety and survival of the more than 200 badly wounded who had been taken into cellars below the headquarters, and the brigade medical officer asked Frost for permission to contact the German commander. The Germans agreed to a truce and everyone laboured throughout the day to remove all the wounded out of the burning building. Then Frost's men dug slit trenches in the gardens of houses, hoping to continue the fight, but the superior numbers of the enemy overwhelmed each group in turn. Many of those British holed up in buildings were also winkled out.

Tony Dean and Alec Milne had been among the first glider pilots to land on Day 1 and had reached Arnhem. They had worried, before Operation Market Garden began, about their landing zone. Throughout their training with The Glider Pilot Regiment they had understood that the value and importance of the regiment was the skills of the pilots to land troops, equipment, arms, vehicles and guns directly on their objective, or at least so close as to create an element of surprise. Yet for 'Market Garden' the planners had decreed that the gliders should land several miles from Arnhem and the objective, the bridge. Now they were leaving the killing ground with its deadly streets and going, with others, to attempt to rejoin airborne comrades in Oosterbeek. Another glider pilot, John Hallower, had been with them but had become separated. He had a traumatic time after fighting ended in Arnhem and played hide-and-seek with the Germans, helped by friendly Dutch folk, for about six months, before being able to return to England and the regiment.

Peter Earle says, with the ever-increasing danger of capture,

Colonel Glover suggested that some of us should try to get back to Oosterbeek. There was a risk but it seemed the best option so, after drawing straws, a group of us began our way back. After a few skirmishes, during which we lost Sergeant Phillips and an infantry lieutenant named Mortimer, our group got through.

When those in Arnhem were taken prisoner the Germans were complimentary about the manner in which the British and their allies had fought the battle, but the officers and men of the British and Allied Airborne forces who had fought so courageously could feel only the bitterness of defeat.

John Frost, later Major-General, was subsequently honoured by the people of Arnhem, who renamed their bridge, 'John Frostbrug'. During the afternoon of 26 September news got through that a withdrawal from Oosterbeek would begin at thirty minutes after midnight. The plan for the withdrawal was for the Royal Artillery, across the river, to begin a supporting barrage while those withdrawing would proceed along a route marked by tapes put in position earlier, and glider pilots would take up positions along the route to act as human signposts. It began to rain heavily before the time for the departure and the ground became very slippery, with bushes, undergrowth and trees dripping water. Captain Matecheck, wounded, had difficulty but, assisted by glider pilots and others, he reached safety. Staff Sergeant Nixon had been with him earlier but they had been parted. Waiting by the river for a boat, they were alarmed when some 25-pounder shells fell close by.

After leaving King's School, Canterbury, which was evacuated to St Austell, Cornwall, where many troops were in training, Alan Kenney joined the army and shortly after his nineteenth birthday he dropped into Oosterbeek with the 1st Parachute Brigade. He tells his story: 'After being held up by intensive fire from automatic weapons and snipers the going got very bloody and through each successive day we fought against great odds, losing many men and growing both very tired and hungry. Eventually, on what proved to be the last evening of the battle, I was wounded in both legs and when the withdrawal began I determined not to wait to be captured but to follow the marked route to the river. Unable to walk, I propelled myself by my hands in a sitting position, dragging my legs behind me.

'After a while pain and exhaustion forced me to give up and I half-lay propped against a tree. Glider pilot Captain Hemmings came along and he managed to carry me on his back along the route, slipping and slithering, to the river and a boat ferrying wounded. The Germans had realised what was going on and were shelling the river: many men were lost, either when boats were sunk or while attempting to swim across to the other side. Back in England I was taken to Netley Hospital, Southampton, where American orderlies used to drive jeeps along corridors.

'My memories of my first and only airborne operation remain strong, among them the fallen soldiers and helping to bury some of them; the smell of blood and dust from the damaged buildings and the noise of bombardment. Many years later, by chance, I was to meet again the officer who saved me.'

Staff Sergeant Alec Davies and Dennis Daniels became separated from other glider pilots and the men of the South Staffordshire Regiment as they tried to get through from Oosterbeek to Arnhem. Then, on the third day, Daniels was killed and Davies went on alone until he met up with glider pilot Douglas Attwell and a South Stafford's private named Ivor Rowberry. The three stayed together until Attwell went off to try to reach the Hartenstein Hotel, and soon afterwards Rowberry was killed. Eventually, hungry and thirsty, Davis called at a house to ask for food and drink and was greeted by Piet and Marit Haas, who offered him shelter. It was at great risk to themselves but they hid him until they were able to pass him on to Dutch patriots. He was moved from successive hiding places, sometimes in damaged buildings, in farm buildings, or in cleverly camouflaged hides in the woods. On one occasion while in such a place he heard the approach of German soldiers, who passed very close to where he was. Finally, with a bicycle and accompanied by a girl, he reached an American unit and safety. After the war, for many years until his death, Alec Davies was a voluntary officer with the Market Garden Veteran's Association.

There were many brave men and women among the Dutch people, among them Jan and Kate Ter Horst, parents of five young children. They lived in a large house with a garden and orchard, and on the second day Kate, in the absence of Jan, who was away assisting the British troops, agreed willingly to allow the house to become a first aid centre, but it soon turned into a very crowded hospital. Kate and her children and some neighbours moved into the cellar. Soon the house became overcrowded with wounded. They occupied beds, stretchers and even the floor, and in time some stretchers had to be placed outside in the garden. Captain Martin of the Royal Army Medical Corps was working flat out, assisted by his orderlies, yet still wounded were being brought in.

Kate Ter Horst related some of her memories: 'Jan, my husband, was away helping the British soldiers. Even in the cellar we could hear the sounds of gunfire and shouts of "Wounded! Wounded!" It was not easy to keep five young children amused or to explain why they were having to remain in the cellar after having enjoyed the freedom of our garden. I would go around the house speaking words of cheer and comfort and reading psalms to soldiers who were little more than boys. They were lying everywhere, in the downstairs rooms, the garden room, in the corridors, under the stairs, even in the lavatory. Upstairs it was the same, every possible space filled. Windows were broken and pieces of glass lay on some of the wounded men. It seemed incredible but my house was sheltering three hundred men!

'In the garden there lay the dead waiting to be buried. The house took a crashing blow when hit by a shell but the doctor and his helpers took no notice. The pain and the suffering was unbelievable; one boy had no legs, another no hands. When I handed round a bottle of fruit juice one man held it for the other to drink. We had no water, the pump in the garden was about twenty metres from the house and a German sniper had it covered. On one occasion a soldier had ventured to the pump and was returning with two buckets full. The sniper fired several shots and made holes in the buckets, letting the water run out. Then as the soldier almost reached the house a bullet hit him.

'I remember the brave way in which the soldiers bore their pain and suffering. I just wanted to comfort them. Finally the day came when a shell hit the house, causing rubble to fall into the cellar, filling it with dust. The doctor was wounded and snipers moved to the orchard and fired into the rooms. Captain Martin, the doctor, was given morphia and as I knew that the Germans would soon be at the house I began to look out clothes for my baby and the other children. That night the withdrawal began, although we did not know it at the time. When morning came there were Germans outside the house and I was told to take my children and what I could carry and leave my house and Oosterbeek. My friends in the cellar had also to go, as well as every other person and child in Oosterbeek. With my five children and some possessions on a handcart I walked to another village to stay with friends. We did not know for how long.'

The failure at Arnhem was unexpected. It was no more than a coincidence that Germany's General Model, one of Hitler's best commanders, had suddenly decided to go to Oosterbeek for a short break from duties. At the same time he had dispersed the elite 2nd SS Panzer Corps to woods around Arnhem for a rest and refitting. When the British gliders began landing and paratroops dropping, the general, taken by surprise, had hastily fled Oosterbeek. Then the Germans had a stroke of luck. To the south, General Student was commanding forces under attack by American airborne forces at Nijmegen and incredibly a complete set of the allies' orders for 'Market Garden' were found by a German soldier in a crashed Waco and taken to the general. By Day 2 General Model also knew of the airborne plan and threw the considerable strength of the SS panzer corps into the battle.

The cost to the Allied force was high. The total casualties among

Allied airborne troops and RAF aircrews was 13,000, and of those The Glider Pilot Regiment lost 230 pilots killed and 500 were wounded or made prisoners of war. Some 2,000 men successfully withdrew on the last night. Many Dutch people also suffered casualties and almost all of the houses were damaged. The Resistance group gave help to the allied troops and many local families gave food and shelter to soldiers seeking to avoid capture. Fifty Dutch people were executed after the British withdrawal and the homes from which the people had been forced to leave were systematically looted. But despite this, through the years Dutch people and their children have maintained an extraordinary closeness with British airborne veterans and their families. Many, many times the glider pilots demonstrated their skills, first as pilots, then as total soldiers, vindicating George Chatterton's insistence that they learn to efficiently use all the arms and equipment the gliders had carried. During the battle glider pilot officers and men became emergency gun crews, machine-gunners and mortar teams. They efficiently handled PIATs and, in small groups, cleared the enemy from their positions, challenging tanks and self-propelled guns.

Eventually, after the Germans had been forced to leave Holland, those airborne men who had been buried in the Ter Horst orchard were exhumed and re-interred, with full military honours, in the military cemetery. Kate Ter Horst and her family returned to their house, and in due course husband Jan became Mayor of Oosterbeek. Very sadly, not long after they returned to their house, one of their children trod on an unsuspected landmine in the garden and was killed.

Through the years many of those who had known Kate during 'Market Garden' returned to see her and her family and were always made welcome. Then, tragically, in 1983 Kate was struck by an out-of-control car by her garden gate and killed. Those wounded men of September 1944 who still survived mourned the loss of their Angel of Oosterbeek.

On the morning of Sunday, 17 September 1944, a fleet of gliders and their tug planes took off from Harwell and together with combinations from other airfields headed for German-occupied Holland. Aboard one Horsa was Roland McFarlane, a young member of a Royal Army Medical Corps team, and they were taking with them a jeep, stretchers and medical supplies. En route over Wiltshire their pilot discovered a technical fault that led him to release from his tug plane and make an emergency landing at Beanacre, near Melksham. While waiting for recovery, all aboard accepted the offers of some local residents to take Sunday lunch with them while the village policeman stood guard over the Horsa and its cargo.

The next day the medics took off again in a replacement glider and flew to Oosterbeek, where the glider pilot, named Castle, made a good landing. After unloading, the RAMC team headed for the Hartenstein Hotel, which had become the Airborne Division headquarters. They set up a Medical Aid Post but during the days that followed casualties became so numerous, with many dead, that the medics had to wait until after dark to move the bodies to an outbuilding near the hotel, for later burial.

When the withdrawal took place the medics remained behind to care for the wounded, and all were taken prisoner by the Germans and transported to Breslau, in Silesia. When the Russian army advanced from the east the Germans took them captive and forced them on what eventually became known as 'The death march', walking through snow and over difficult terrain for several hundred miles, with the Russians getting closer. The more able helped those who were less able but many of the prisoners died on the journey. The survivors eventually reached Munich, Bavaria, where American troops met them and released them from their captors. The Americans cared for them until it was possible for them to be repatriated to England.

When the withdrawal was under way I was fortunately able to assist a young corporal paratrooper who had been badly wounded. He had bravely attempted to reach safety but had collapsed. With my assistance he eventually reached the Lower

Rhine and the comparative safety of a boat that took him and other wounded men across the river.

John Bright had been wounded and was a patient in Queen Wilhelmina Hospital when the Germans arrived and told everyone they were prisoners. After a journey by road everyone was put aboard a train in very crowded conditions, but Bright managed to escape during the journey; only three others were able enough to go with him, the rest were too badly wounded. After rolling down an embankment the four men walked across country seeking what cover they could, until they reached a farm. It was late in the day so they hid until morning and revealed themselves when the farmer appeared at dawn. He proved to be an Allied sympathiser and a member of the Dutch Resistance and took the four men into the farmhouse where they were given a hot breakfast. The escapees remained at the farm for a week, during which time members of the Dutch Resistance called to talk to them, promising to move them elsewhere when it was safe to do so. The farmer and his wife produced civilian clothing and at last came the time for two of the airborne men to move elsewhere.

John Bright and another were taken, wearing the civilian suits over their uniforms, towards the next 'safe' house but on the way they saw some Germans ahead. Their female escort immediately pushed them into an orchard and bade both men not to utter a word and to act normally when they reached the main road. On the road, with Bright's arm linked with the woman's and the other man walking with them, they passed German troops unmolested. Crossing a canal bridge, they reached the premises of a coal merchant, who took them to a shed by a coke store and opened a panel that admitted them to a small hiding place containing beds, table and chairs and washing facilities. Each night they were able to emerge to enjoy a meal with the coal merchant and his family.

Their next move came a week later when they were supplied with bicycles and told to follow two Dutch cyclists. At a railway crossing the first two Dutchmen turned off and another cyclist took over as the leader. Then, after a few miles, they reached a house, where Bright was parted from his escapee comrade and taken off on his own for what proved to be a 15-mile ride, during which they passed a great many German vehicles with men aboard them. Once again, at a pre-arranged spot, the Dutchman guiding Bright changed places with another; soon afterwards his new Dutch friend brought him to a town, where they stopped and the guide asked whether Bright would like a haircut. While putting a wrap around John's shoulders the barber caught a glimpse of the uniform underneath his suit, but he made no comment and when the time came for payment he would take no money, but murmured 'Good luck'.

Taken to a mill where workers were busy, Bright was first given a meal and then allowed to bath. The mill-owner and his wife, though, could offer no accommodation because there were already a number of British soldiers in hiding there; instead he was taken to another house, where three Allied aircrew who had been shot down were already hiding, and John Bright remained there for two weeks, where, within a small area, more than 300 Allied servicemen were being hidden and the Dutch Resistance was completing plans to get them all to safety. When the night came for the evacuation every one of the escapees was assembled in the grounds of a mental hospital and told the plan for their mass exodus. A British aircraft would deliver some arms and ammunition, not enough for everyone but sufficient to help them if trouble arose. Just before midnight they were assembled on a bank of the River Rhine and told that at midnight troops on the other side would fire tracer bullets to indicate the place from which rescue boats would set out. The escapees finally got across the river, where they were met and given food. From there they were taken into Belgium to await repatriation to England.

Jan de Ritter was 12 years old at the time of the battle and he recalls that there were very many aircraft flying overhead, fighter planes, bombers, tug planes and gliders. He was living near barracks from which German forces destroyed many in the air. Later, in Arnhem, the Germans cut off the water supply to prevent the Allied troops from getting any. The action also meant that whenever buildings caught fire, and the instances were many, there was no water to bring the flames under control. One day he saw a long column of Allied prisoners being marched along a road and suddenly, from a house, a sniper opened fire and killed two glider pilots. The column immediately halted, the leaders protesting to their guards. Then a German officer appeared and shouted an order through a window; the sniper emerged, and as he did so the German officer drew a pistol and shot him dead.

Brigadier Tom Haddon had mixed feelings about gliders and his experiences reveal why. When second in command of The Border Regiment he flew with his battalion by Horsa to Sicily but was in one of the 47 gliders that were forced to land in the sea. He swam ashore to join his battalion, found them and fought with them gallantly. For Operation Market Garden he flew from Bradwell as Battalion Commander but the glider he was in suffered a broken tow rope while still over England and the pilot had to make an emergency landing. Undeterred, Tom organised another glider to fly him and his HQ staff to Arnhem, but while flying over Belgium the tug plane was shot down and the glider pilot was forced to make a landing. Not to be outdone, Haddon made his way towards Holland, passed through 30 Corps lines and met up with the Polish Parachute Regiment at Driel. He later crossed the River Rhine with the 4th Dorset Regiment in an attempt to reach his battalion, which was fighting in Oosterbeek. However, while attempting to get through the German lines he was captured and became a prisoner of war.

Lieutenant Colonel S.C. Griffith related a story concerning another glider pilot whom he came upon assisting a wounded paratrooper.

The para had been wounded by an exploding mortar bomb and a splinter had passed through the front of his neck and out of the back. His windpipe had been severed and he could not breathe properly. The glider pilot, named Paget, realising that the man was near death, took a fountain pen from a pocket, removed the cap protecting the nib and neatly cut the closed end off, thus making a short tube. He made an incision below the wound, inserted the tube and the para began to breathe again.

Staff Sergeant Reg Dance saw active service in France in 1940 and got back to England with the help of two amateur sailors in a small sailing boat. He was one of the earliest volunteers to The Glider Pilot Regiment, with whom he went to North Africa in 1943. He then flew a Waco, with Sergeant Barker as his co-pilot to Sicily, but was released too soon and had to ditch in the sea. He later took part in the D-Day operations and Operation Market Garden. He was badly wounded while fighting in Oosterbeek and was later taken prisoner by the Germans. After some local treatment, he was taken to various prison camps, his back wound being continually troublesome. In early 1945 Russian troops reached the camp he was in, but the Allied prisoners were little better off, as they were roughly treated and kept on almost starvation rations as they were moved hundreds of miles, under armed escort, eastwards through Silesia and part of Poland. There Reg was carried by comrades to a lorry, which took them to a train that carried them, in dreadful conditions, to Odessa, from where the prisoners sailed back to Britain. It was the end of Reg's military service, as he was found to be medically unfit and released from the army.

Two others who served with distinction during Operation Market Garden were Kenneth Shipman and Alec Shepherd. Ken was severely wounded and taken prisoner. Repatriated in 1945, he received further hospital treatment before rejoining The Glider Pilot Regiment. Alec, too, was badly wounded and after hospital treatment was declared unfit for further service. He later took up a teaching post in a school in Jersey, Channel Islands, becoming its headmaster.

Other bizarre happenings during the Arnhem battle are reported:

Glider pilot Richard Forester was in a small group repelling a series of German attacks, during which he was wounded in the right arm and shoulder. Later, in a hospital, he saw British and

German medical officers and their orderlies working together, attending to the many wounded while the battle continued.

During the fighting, Staff Sergeant Michael Long, a tall young glider pilot, found himself face to face with a German soldier. Both fired their pistols simultaneously. The shot from Long hit the German, whose shot hit Michael in the leg, causing him to lose his balance. The German seized his opportunity and leapt upon the glider pilot, pinning him to the ground. Then, he and Long dressed each other's wounds.

The Horsa piloted by two Richards – Adams and Ennis – was carrying two jeeps and trailers loaded with ammunition, plus some Royal Artillery personnel. After releasing from their tug plane and going down towards the landing zone, a German ack-ack shell exploded close to the port side of the glider, causing it to buck. At the same time, Richard Adams, who was at the controls, slumped in his seat, mortally wounded. Richard Ennis took the controls of the Horsa, which was almost down, but it hit some trees, causing Ennis to be thrown out through the perspex of the cockpit, still strapped in his seat. At the same time the two jeeps and loaded trailers burst into the cockpit.

From the garden of his house in Bedhampton, Mark Somers looked up at planes and gliders. He recognised the gliders as Horsas because of his employment as an engineering draughts-man at Airspeed Limited, Portsmouth.

'I was closely involved with both their design and the prototypes that preceded the War Office order for the production of the Horsa, and it was a particular thrill to see so many in the air. My nephew, Eric Lowe, had been a glider pilot too, although sadly he was killed in a flying accident not long before D-Day.'

During the withdrawal Rob Cole, of the Army Medical Corps, was on the far bank of the river waiting to give assistance to walking wounded as they came ashore. In the darkness he heard someone in the water and then a soldier appeared, swimming with laboured strokes towards the bank.

'When he reached the shallow water and I assisted him ashore he flopped to the ground until his laboured breathing eased. After a brief rest he got to his feet, grinned, and asked the way to Kings Cross. Then bootless he set off cheerfully towards those who would give him a meal and new footwear. He was one happy glider pilot!'

It has often been asked why Operation Market Garden failed. Had it been successful it could have changed the course of history. The reason was that those responsible for the planning believed that enemy guns were too formidable to allow airborne troops to land close to the objective and also that the area close to Arnhem was unsuitable for gliders to land. Thus the distance that the glider-borne troops had to cover was too great.

It also seems certain that though the Dutch Underground had given accurate information of enemy locations, it was either ignored or misunderstood.

Since the end of World War II Arnhem has retained an affectionate place in the hearts of those who fought and survived the battle and many of them, with families of those killed, make an annual pilgrimage to Arnhem, Oosterbeek and Nijmegen. The Dutch people have an enduring friendship that has continued through the younger generations of those who welcomed the airborne troops in 1944.

A monument, consisting of a piece of a stone column from a battle-ruined building, bears the simple inscription '17 September 1944' and every year a procession marches slowly there to lay wreaths. The Hartenstein Hotel, is now the Dutch airborne Museum.

During a reunion visit to Arnhem, as house guests of the family

Kortlang, my wife and I were taken to a small town an hour's drive from Arnhem called Den Dungen which has maintained a special relationship with The Glider Pilot Regiment. Two pilots of the regiment, Daniel Griffiths and 'Skip' Evans, sought refuge in the town and were kept hidden, at very great risk to those who gave them shelter and sustenance, as the German army were in occupation.

The townsfolk have insured that the memory of those glider pilots is kept alive by naming a street Pilotenstraat.

E.M. d'Hondt is a great friend of The Glider Pilot Regiment and of all veterans of 'Market Garden', as indeed are all the people of Nijmegen, of which he is Mayor. There are still townsfolk who risked their lives to assist glider pilots and others to escape from the area, rather than let them become prisoners of war.

The Germans turned off the main water supply early in the battle to try to force a surrender. For their own troops they used mobile water tankers.

All these years afterwards, pictures of Arnhem still slip unbidden into my mind. To have been there was an experience never to be forgotten. The fires, falling masonry, the explosions, the echo of guns and the dreadful chatter of automatic weapons. Men lying in the stillness of death, wounded men walking dazedly, many propped against whatever support they could find or just lying, contorted, on the ground.

Together we had gone through months and months of training to prepare us for what we were experiencing, but for many it had all ended. Courage was in evidence wherever one looked – there were heroes everywhere, but not enough medals for them all.

The versatilty, flexibility and confidence of glider pilots was revealed many times. A particular example was that of Staff Sergeant R.F. Tilley, who took command of the 7th battalion of the King's Own Scottish Borderers during the battle of Arnhem after their officers had all been killed or seriously wounded. Tilley was awarded a Distinguished Conduct Medal for this initiative.

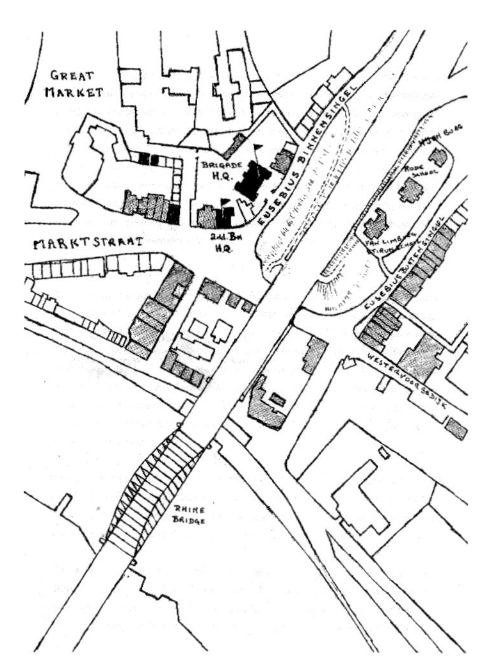

The Arnhem Bridge area showing brigade H.Q.

The bridge at Arnhem now.

19

Return to the Rhine

Operation Varsity, 24–25 March 1945

Although the Allied advance had been delayed by the Germans, who were fighting tenaciously, the allied commanders looked again at the Rhine, in particular at the stretch of the river south-east of Arnhem, near Wesel, above the important industrial region of Germany's Ruhr.

The plan for 'Varsity' would not be dependent upon a single bridge but included an amphibious operation on a 20 mile stretch of the River Rhine in combination with airborn force British and American and glider-borne forces. The airborne force, the British 1st and 6th and the United States 17th and 82nd Airborne Divisions, comprised 40,000 paratroops and air-landing troops, with access to aircraft belonging to two Royal Air Force groups and one American Air Force wing.

General Brereton chaired a meeting at the War Office during which Colonel Chatterton, Commander Glider Pilots learned that two complete airborne divisions were to drop simultaneously on the east bank of the river at Hamminkeln, five or six miles north of Wesel, while the British 21st Army Group were to make an assault across the river at a point where it is a quarter of a mile wide. The general plan was that the British 2nd Army and the American 9th army would cross the Rhine on the left and right respectively to capture the Communication Centre of Wesel and move northward to enable the river to be bridged at Emmerich.

Eastward and northeast a bridgehead would be established from which further offensive operations could be developed. The 21st Army Group were to position themselves east of the Rhine and north of the Ruhr so that operations could be developed quickly to penetrate deep into Germany.

That ground operation was code-named 'Plunder'. In addition, the largest airborne lift by gliders in history would be made. Colonel Chatterton was faced with the need to bring his glider force to full strength in a very short time. He had abandoned his firm conviction that glider pilots should also be superb fighting soldiers and had accepted trained pilots from the Royal Air Force Reserve and together with the veterans of Arnhem they now faced up to the prospect of battle.

The Germans had learned the lesson of massed-glider attack at Arnhem. There they soon realised that glider forces unloading were vulnerable to quite small numbers of troops and mobile units had been formed, capable of rushing to the scene of a massed landing immediately after receiving the alarm. In the view of the German High Command, it was vital to attack air-landing troops immediately, to disrupt their preparations for battle and to cause casualties. By so doing larger forces could prepare counter-measures to render air landings ineffective.

The number of gliders to be used for the Rhine crossing required 880 pilots to fly 440 gliders, less than the total number used at Arnhem over a number of days, but enough to comprise the largest single lift ever.

The RAF pilots were given conversion courses on Hotspur, Horsa and Hamilcar gliders and a 14-day course on the use of small arms, plus a week on assault courses. Colonel Chatterton decided to match rank with rank; the wings remaining under the command of their army commanders, but the command of the squadrons being equally divided between majors and squadron leaders and flights between captains and flight lieutenants. Whenever possible, crews were made up of one army and one RAF pilot.

This enabled the ex-RAF pilots to become versed in army methods.

The build-up for Operation Varsity was now ready; the Royal Air Force and American aircraft for towing the gliders and carrying paratroops were assembled in East Anglia on various airfields. The 14,000 men of the airborne divisions who were to take part, either as glider-borne troops or paratroopers, would at all times be within the range of the guns of 21st Army Group and would be landed, close to the objectives, before the Germans could assess their intention. Re-supply aircraft would not be required. The General Officer Commanding 6th Airborne Division, Major General Bois, decided that the British gliders would make tactical landings instead of a massed landing, an idea put forward by the Commander Glider Pilots, which meant that the gliders would descend directly on top of the enemy at points decided upon by the commander concerned, while fitting in with the overall plan. This method of streaming was practised and rehearsed by the glider pilots assiduously.

It was realised that gliders were most vulnerable during the time between releasing from the tug plane and landing, because they provided large and relatively slow targets. At Arnhem gliders were hit innumerable times while in the air. Thus surprise was vital, with the time between release and landing reduced as much as possible.

New modified gliders too, with loads rolling straight out of the nose, reduced the time spent unloading. Prudently, the rear-unloading system was retained as an alternative in case the nose became jammed on landing. The improved Horsa could also carry an additional weight of 250 pounds. That meant that as an alternative to carrying 28 fully equipped soldiers, it could carry either two 5-hundredweight vehicles, or one vehicle and a 75-mm gun with crew and ammunition.

Another planning alteration was that, instead of going into action before the ground forces, the air landing was to be made ahead of the advanced formations after the river crossings.

The airborne troops were briefed to capture high ground forming the western edge of the Diersfordter Wald in order to neutralise the infantry and artillery positioned there, to prevent them causing havoc with the assault forces on the lower ground. Two road bridges and a railway bridge over the Issel had also to be captured, to provide access for the main Allied breakthrough into Germany. The Glider Pilot Regiment's task was to land 6th Air Landing Brigade at Hamminkeln. The brigade consisted of the 2nd Battalion the Oxford and Buckinghamshire Light Infantry; 1st Battalion the Ulster Rifles; 12th Battalion the Devonshire Regiment; 53rd Light Regiment Royal Artillery; 3rd and 4th Air Landing Anti-tank Batteries RA; the airborne Armoured Reconnaissance Regiment and units of the Royal Engineers and Field Ambulance.

Paratroops of the 3rd and 5th Parachute Brigades were also briefed to land in the area. A *coup de main* party of men from the Oxfordshire and Buckinghamshire Light Infantry and the Royal Ulster Rifles, carried by 15 gliders, were detailed to capture the three River Issel bridges and to prepare them for demolition in case of a German counter-attack. Intelligence reports had shown that none of the landing zones were planted with anti-invasion poles and that the ground was both firm and level.

The Allies also knew that there were ten German divisions within a 20-mile radius of the assault area and that they numbered some 50,000 men, with tanks and self-propelled guns. Also the 1st Parachute Army, supported by two infantry divisions of hardened combatants, were defending Wesel and its immediate area. A week prior to the operation a rehearsal flight to test navigational aids took place. Code-named Operation Token, it involved 12 Horsa gliders and tug planes flying from Earls Colne, balasted with concrete. The destination was the Xanten area of the Rhine. They were escorted by high-altitude fighter planes and all returned safely, without incident, Whether it alerted the Germans to the pending large airborne assault can only be guessed at.

On 24 March 1945, in perfect flying conditions, 400 Horsas and Hamilcars, led by Lieutenant-Colonel Iain Murray, took off between 0600 hours and 0750 hours, bound for the River Rhine. At the same time 900 Waco gliders carrying American troops took off from France. For days and nights troops and equipment moved towards the assault sector, on the ground, in a great invasion build-up similar to that of D-Day. Among the mass of equipment entailed were 4,000 tank-transporters, and eight times that number of vehicles. There were amphibious tanks and naval landing craft hauled to the sector on 24-wheeled trailers and convoys of vehicles transported pontoons and bridging sections. All this leads one to think that the Germans must have guessed at what was going to happen. Add to all the foregoing thousands of tons of ammunition, petrol and other stores, and one has to assume that the Germans were aware of the massive build-up on the west side of the river.

A particular German defence feature was an area of high wooded ground north-west of Wesel, known as the Diersfordter Wald, in an otherwise flat and featureless area. Troops and guns on the height therefore dominated the river and the flat area to the west and provided a protective ridge to the smaller River Issels' three bridges to the east, as well as the town of Hamminkeln. That was the objective of the airborne army. Unlike at Arnhem, the entire airborne operation at Wesel would go down in successive landings over a period of four hours.

The operation brief stressed the need for the German anti-aircraft defences to be suppressed before General Brereton's forces arrived and the small town of Wesel to be subjected to heavy bombing. In the event the anti-aircraft defences were far from suppressed, and the bombardment of Wesel, together with a smokescreen put up by Allied ground forces, had resulted in a dense smoke-like haze that obliterated much of the target area and recognisable landmarks by the time the gliders arrived at the landing zone.

The tactical landings called for the Horsas, carrying the Oxford and Buckinghamshire Light Infantry, to land at 1020 hours to capture one road bridge and the rail bridge, followed by 58 Horsas carrying men of the Air Landing Brigade three minutes later. At the same time the Horsas carrying the Royal Ulsters were to land and one was hit by flak. Then it was hit again and lost bits of the Horsa, including the flaps. Some of the platoon being carried were wounded but none of them seriously, and immediately the glider landed and came to a halt they scrambled out. As they were leaving the Horsa a German machine-gun opened up, wounding the officer leading the platoon. He was left behind with two or three others but the rest of the men went off and did their bit in the battle.

A Hamilcar carrying a tank, crew and ammunition was hit by flak as it went down towards the landing zone, bits of it being lost. Despite this, ex-RAF Flight Lieutenant Love, assisted by his co-pilot Sergeant McEwan, got the huge glider down but because the hydraulics were smashed it careered at speed across the ground until it ran into a ditch. The men scrambled out and began to dig in as a German machine-gun opened up. Eventually they were able to unload the tank and move off to take part in the action.

Lieutenant Sydney St John approached the landing zone after the long tow. It was his first operation, having joined The Glider Pilot Regiment late in the war after serving with the Royal Artillery Coastal Command. After releasing he descended through a hail of bullets but landed safely and with a platoon of the Oxfordshire and Buckinghamshire Light Infantry took part in the action. Years afterwards, in a Fleet Street hostelry, in company with ex-glider pilots 'Holly' Hollingdale and myself, he recounted the surprise of Colonel Chatterton that he was 32 when he volunteered for the regiment.

Three thousand feet above the smokescreened River Issel, Captain Boucher-Giles made a steep turn to starboard then, as he took his glider down, machine-gun fire raked the aircraft, some of it went through the floor of the cockpit between the captain and his co-pilot, Sergeant Garland, without hitting either. He put on half-flap, which did not work, and he realised it had been damaged. Visibility was almost nil and Hamminkeln was completely obscured. They made a soft landing in a ploughed field and everyone got out unhurt, although they were under attack from mortars and small-arms fire. A sniper was active from a nearby building and the glider boys returned fire with their automatic weapons, peppering all the windows, and eventually the German activity stopped and all was quiet.

During a lull the men unloaded the glider and it was almost completed when the captain was shot. Sergeant Garland carried him into a shallow depression, dressed his wound and gave him morphine to ease the pain, then had to leave him, to take part in the action.

A remarkable achievement was that of Sergeant Major Leslie Turnbull, who was awarded the Conspicuous Gallantry Medal, the only such award to a soldier during World War II.

The Colonel of the Oxfordshire and Buckinghamshire Light Infantry was a passenger in a Horsa piloted by Squadron Leader Reynolds, who made his approach to the landing zone by the railway station, under heavy anti-aircraft fire. A gunsight was close to the station and Reynolds landed between two of the guns, and those aboard the Horsa attacked the battery and captured it.

Staff Sergeant 'Nobby' Clarke flew towards his landing zone while being shot at by ack-ack fire. He was carrying a captain and a platoon of the Devonshire Regiment and landed between the river and an anti-aircraft gun emplacement. Clarke and the others raced from the Horsa and attacked the surprised gunners, before sabotaging the guns and taking some prisoners.

Gliders were descending thick and fast and most landed close to their objectives, despite the ack-ack and small-arms fire. Those gliders detailed for the *coup de main* attack on the bridges landed with pinpoint accuracy and the bridges were quickly captured and held. Platoon Leader Captain Mike Smith, Ox and Bucks, said,

'As our Horsa approached the ground we could see the Rhine shining through a small gap in the smoke-haze, but the ground, as we neared it, was completely obscured. However, our pilot put us down close to the spot detailed in our brief and we were able to immediately go into action.'

Staff Sergeant Roy Howard, Flight NCO 'B' Squadron and a veteran of the *coup-de-main* operation at the River Orne, piloted a MK2 Horsa, with ex-RAF Flying Officer Daniels as his second pilot. The flight to Germany was uneventful but with all the smoke hiding the ground, plus a lot of flak, the landing, in Roy's words, 'was a bit hairy' and he was glad to get the glider on to the ground, unload and send the load on its way without damage or loss. Then followed five busy days on the ground near Hamminkeln, after which 'B' Squadron returned to Down Ampney, via Eindhoven.

Major Tod Sweeney, Oxfordshire and Buckinghamshire Light Infantry, was also a veteran of Operation Deadstick, the pre-D-Day assault on the bridges over Caen Canal and the River Orne. Then he had been a subaltern platoon leader, now he was on the headquarters staff. When the Horsa 1 was released, the pilot had to get down through the thick dust-smoke and he circled around looking for the landing zone. Other gliders were doing the same thing and it made them easy targets for German ack-ack gunners, who were not affected visually by the smoke layer as they laid their guns on the targets by instruments. When Sweeney's glider landed, the jeep and other cargo were unloaded under attack from small-arms fire and he got his men into firing positions until all the gliders were down. Some of them were carrying mortar bombs and petrol which could, at any time, have gone up like fireballs.

The major's battalion began the operation with 600 men but suffered heavy losses – 110 being killed and a much larger number wounded. During the night they were attacked by the Germans, but the next day the 52nd Lowland Division arrived and relieved them.

Flying in a Hamilcar carrying a Tetrarch tank and its crew, plus shells and automatic ammunition, was Lieutenant Starkey. 'After crossing the Rhine, casting off and landing, the tank rolled out of the glider and the crew was soon in action. I saw a glider come down, very fast, and after landing it tipped forward and crashed. We could not stop to see whether there were any survivors.'

Staff Sergeant Jenkins took his glider down, blinded and lost in the smoke, guided only by the compass readings of his second pilot, Sergeant Anderson. Then, through a clear patch, Jenkins saw a church spire. At 600 feet he put on full flap and went down, now able to see the white gravestones in the churchyard. He landed in a ploughed field and dived for cover as everyone began to leave the glider under heavy fire; two soldiers were killed as they attempted to do so.

Staff Sergeant Pearton's Horsa was hit by automatic fire as it touched down and began to roll forward, the bullets raking the portside and killing four of the troops and wounding others. When the Horsa's forward run stopped, those who were unhurt left the glider quickly and took cover while they assessed the situation. Four medical orderlies, with stretchers, raced to the glider to give help to the wounded. 'They were successful in getting the lads out and began to carry them towards cover when a burst from a machine-gun cut down one pair.'

The pilots of 'C' Squadron were briefed by Major Dale, the Squadron Commander, who told them that 'with the whole British and American Tactical Air Forces in support, nothing can go wrong'. That conjecture did not foresee the sickening sight of one Hamilcar lurching to destruction just as its pilot came into sight of the Rhine.

'E' Squadron took off in their Horsas from RAF Birch, in Essex, some of them carrying men and equipment of the Oxfordshire and Buckinghamshire Light Infantry, and others of the Royal Ulster Rifles. The 60 gliders, in a clear sky, crossed the Channel and as they got within sight of the Rhine they were greeted by flak and those glider pilots further back saw some of the Dakota tug planes return home bullet-ridden. Close to the release point, 20-mm Oerlikons and some heavier guns were firing and many of the shells were incendiary, which set some gliders alight. Like everyone else, the pilots of 'E' Squadron were handicapped by the smoke covering the ground, and the gliders were circling looking for clues to enable them to land safely. The road east of Hamminkeln could be seen faintly and the railway too. The pilots knew from their briefings that both sides of the railway were lined by trees. One glider going in to land had a wing blown off. Pilots and troops landing in that area came face to face with German troops approaching from the River Issel, accompanied by a half-track, which was forced to retreat when one of the Ox and Bucks men fired a PIAT. The German troops went with it, apparently having no stomach for further action.

Further along the railway line was the rendezvous for glider pilots and they found that some of the infantrymen had taken prisoners. The Germans were marched to Hamminkeln, which was in the control of the Devonshire Regiment. The glider pilots were then ordered to take up positions in the front line, with the Germans only some 200 yards distance across the River Issel. During the night there was a steady exchange of shots between the opposing sides until suddenly, the Second Army began a bombardment to prevent the Germans from sending in more troops.

When the bombardment stopped, a German Tiger tank, followed by troops attempted to cross a bridge and a sharp battle ensued. Both sides suffered heavy losses and eventually Royal Engineers blew up the bridge to prevent the Germans taking it. Later, British tanks reached the area and with the help of a further bombardment from second Army guns, the glider pilots were able to leave their forward position. On Monday, 26 March, they were moved to Eindhoven and the following day returned to England.

The Royal Ulster Rifles' task was to seize key terrain in a bridgehead area east of the Rhine in support of ground forces making an assault river crossing. The Ulsters were a glider-borne unit of 6th Air Landing Brigade, and on 24 March, after landing from the gliders that took them to the battle area, they attacked and captured a bridge over the River Issel that was some 200 yards from a railway level crossing. Their mortar officer, Dickie Sweet, was in a glider that was shot up before it landed; but despite the odds against it he reached the bridge, although a little late.

Confused by the thick acrid smoke-haze obscuring the ground and vital landmarks, several gliders had been landed some distance from their landing zone and the pilots conferred while working out where they were while their passengers unloaded. Marching off on a compass bearing towards the River Issel, they met some American airborne men, who joined up with them. Travelling in one of the gliders was Peter Hutton of *Picture Post*, a popular magazine. He later wrote that they heard German tanks approaching, which soon came into view, but travelled across the front of the airborne groups without stopping, which was just as well as the Allied party had only small arms and light automatics. The glider pilots and those with them eventually reached their objective, to find many dead and wounded Americans who had dropped there in error and been shot up, both in the air and on the ground, by German machine-guns and mortars. It was American practice for paratroops to drop in bunches, which left them vulnerable to attack. The British, in contrast, dropped spaced out, thus providing a more difficult target. The wounded were given what help the glider pilots and the others could provide.

Pilots of The Glider Pilot Regiment flying Hamilcars had delivered a troop with a 17-pounder that immediately went into action and repelled German tanks in face of a determined onslaught. Later, when the bridges had been secured, the advancing British and American support troops pressed the Germans back and the Allied bridgehead expanded.

Staff Sergeant Sotiris Antonopoulos, who had survived 11 days in a dinghy with other glider pilots in the Bay of Biscay in 1943, piloted a Horsa loaded with a trailer of ammunition, an officer and 15 men of the Royal Ulster Rifles. He had to contend, like the other pilots, with the smoke-haze obscuring the ground below, but made a landing while under fire from machine-guns. Taking cover after landing, they then saw some Americans and joined them. Together they made their way to the rendezvous at Hamminkeln railway station, taking some prisoners on the way. The officer and men of the Royal Ulster Rifles headed off towards their objective and left Antonopoulos and his co-pilot, Sergeant Gosney, in charge of the prisoners. They decided to march them along the railway track, but then, finding an infantry officer, they handed them over.

I flew a Horsa carrying a platoon of the 2nd Battalion the Royal Ulster Rifles and as we approached our release point the Halifax towing us rocked and then banked as shells exploded in coloured bursts, and at the end of the towline my Horsa bucked. The men behind me were quiet but I guessed that they must have been wondering what was happening. For my part I was perspiring heavily as I strove to hold the Horsa level and Dickie Forster my co-pilot, sat white and tense. Then, only a moment after we had released, I heard him gasp in horror as the Halifax ahead exploded in a great crimson flash and flaming fragments began to fall earthward. The sight was sickening.

I got the Horsa down in controlled turns through the smoke-haze with bullets and shells exploding all round. We went straight down onto the German army and it was no picnic. My landing was uneven and my starboard wing tipped towards the ground and broke off. A wheel had been damaged by a shell fragment while we were in the air, causing the bad landing. Other gliders were landing all round us, some very badly damaged and one dug its nose into the ground, causing it to turn over onto its back, killing and wounding all aboard. At the end of the second day, with the battle won, we were withdrawn to Eindhoven, then returned to England and a period of rest in Devonshire.

An anti-tank gunner, Roger Black, was in a Hamilcar. 'When it released from its tug plane it was just one of a great many gliders all seemingly in the same piece of sky. Our pilot had to go down through thick smoke, circling around as he tried to locate his landing zone.' When Black's glider landed and they began to unload they came under fire from a machine-gun and the men got under cover. Other gliders were coming down; one was carrying petrol and when it was hit it exploded into a fireball.

When a platoon of the Oxfordshire and Buckinghamshires left the Horsa they were pinned down for a while by a German machine-gun, but then an infantryman who had played cricket for Bedfordshire in the Minor League hurled a grenade some 20 yards or so and put the enemy gunners out of action. The platoon, led by a lieutenant and accompanied by the glider pilots, then proceeded to the Issel, where they linked up with paratroops.

Soon after landing his Horsa, Pilot Officer Alexander 'Sandy' Royle was wounded in the right knee and was unable to walk. The leg became very swollen and painful and he slit the blood-sodden trouser leg to ease the constriction. Paratroops had dropped nearby and the enemy had shot a number as they descended. One parachutist had dropped into a tree and as he struggled to free himself was shot dead. Sandy was eventually found by two medical orderlies, one of whom had a blood-soaked bandage round his head. With great courage they dressed Royle's wounds and took him to a first aid post and he was eventually airlifted to England where, at RAF Wroughton Hospital, his leg was amputated above the knee.

Glider pilot Tom Bourne was a very proud member of The Glider Pilot Regiment and flew Horsas to both Arnhem and to Germany for the Rhine crossing. For the latter he took off from Rivenhall carrying a platoon of the Royal Ulster Rifles. Visibility was good as they rendezvoused above Hawkinge with formations from other airfields. Some tug planes towed two gliders flying almost wing-tip to wing-tip and Tom Bourne wondered what were the thoughts of those in the gliders as sometimes the wing-tips seemed very close together. Over Belgium the formation was joined by American gliders. Approaching the landing zone

Bourne was aware of the crack, crack of machine-gun fire, accompanied by shell bursts. He got the glider down through the thick smoke obscuring the ground. There were Germans among the landing gliders and they seemed to be disoriented. One glider crashed beside Bourne's glider and all aboard were killed, which added to the confusion.

Disorientated by the thick, acrid smoke that obscured vital landmarks the pilot of one glider had to land some distance from the landing zone. While the pilots worked out where they were, their airborne passengers calmly unloaded before leaving with the pilots on a compass bearing. On the way they were joined by several Americans.

When war was declared Robert Dainty was serving with the Royal Rhodesian Police Force but quickly volunteered to join the army and was soon in England. Now, as a captain, he was travelling in a glider that was giving its passengers a bumpy ride as they approached the landing zone, due to air turbulence created by the many tug planes in the area. 'However, our pilot, Staff Sergeant Roberts, got us down in a series of turns despite the enemy flak bursting around us. After landing we quickly disembarked and unloaded but came under fire from an automatic and small-arms fire. This caused us casualties; my corporal was killed and two or three of the men became walking wounded.

'On reaching our objective, where we found many dead and badly wounded, we again came under attack, but we responded in good spirit. With the later arrival on the scene of our support troops the enemy, realising that they were outnumbered by a superior force, began to retreat with some haste.'

Monty Modlin, of the BBC, reported the sickening sight of a Horsa approaching its landing zone and when almost down it was hit at point-blank range by a German 88-mm gun. There were no survivors.

Later he visited a casualty station set up in a house, where medical officers and their medical teams were working flat out tending to and operating on men brought in from a nearby aid post and from the battle area, some of whom were glider pilots. One man, a Canadian paratrooper, was very badly burned and Monty learned that when a glider had landed it was fired upon by an automatic while the men being carried were still inside. Realising that the construction of the Horsa gave the men no protection, the Canadian ran towards it and attempted to throw a smoke grenade between it and the enemy. His throw was hindered by a part of the glider; the grenade had rolled back, exploded and thrown molten phosphorus onto him. Modlin remained at the casualty station until British support troops began to arrive.

The daylight assault meant that the Allied glider-borne troops and parachutists were met by German infantry and armour that had been alerted of their coming with devastating results. For some reason, though, the German High Command held back support troops, thus giving the Allies time to hold out in face of a determined series of attacks by German infantry and armour. RAF Tempests proved superior to the Germans aeroplanes, and US Liberators were able to successfully fly in supplies, which were dropped from a low altitude to ensure that they landed where they were wanted, although that did make them targets for German gun crews.

Many Liberators were being hit, causing them either to explode in the air or crash. Those that did complete their mission and were able to return to base raced to collect the supplies for the next drops, using every means possible to carry them to the battle area as quickly as possible.

The Allied airborne assault was a complete success and on the second day the German resistance ended. Casualties on both sides were high and today the Reichwald Cemetery is the last resting place of the many British, Canadian and American troops who were killed only six weeks before the end of the war in Europe.

The heavy pall of smoke above the ground had made things very difficult for the glider pilots and paratroops and there were subsequently a number of theories as to the cause. The most popular one was that the extremely heavy bombing by the Royal Air Force on Wesel, combined with the heavy artillery bombardment preceding the airborne landings, had created a great volume of smoke that was added to by dust clouds from the rubble resulting from the attack. A less popular theory was that the Allies had laid a smokescreen prior to the landings to cover the movements of the Allied airborne troops and that the wind lifted it upwards, screening the ground from the air. Certainly the smoke proved to be a hazard that the glider pilots had to overcome.

The training and the skills of the pilots contributed largely to the success of the operation, and American General Ridgeway subsequently wrote:

The airborne assault preceding the Rhine crossing destroyed German guns and rear defensive positions in the first twenty four hours, defensive positions it might have taken conventional ground forces very many days to overcome. The impact of the airborne divisions shattered the hostile enemy defences and allowed a prompt link-up with the ground troops. The increased bridgehead materially assisted the build-up for subsequent success, permitting the Allied armoured units to debouch into the North German plain at full strength and with great momentum. Glider pilots in particular displayed considerable flying skills, bravery and military expertise.

There were many heroic, tragic and bizarre happenings during the operation:

In one glider were a commanding officer and his headquarters staff. As the glider carrying them approached the landing zone the pilot was killed and his co-pilot immediately took over the controls. Then, as he was descending, he too was hit by shrapnel from a shell-burst and slumped dead in his seat. A sergeant on the colonel's staff, with no flying experience, pushed the dead pilot to one side and grabbed the controls. Somehow he landed the glider safely but did not know how to stop it, so it ran on and on until it at last came to rest, with all aboard safe.

On the ground, after disembarking, a glider pilot was hit by a bullet that went through his helmet, passed through his skull and out of the other side of his helmet. Yet when found by a medical orderly he was still conscious.

Glider pilot Nigel Brown had a Bren gun shot out of his hands by a German tank's heavy machine-gun. Victor Peters, another pilot, was thrown clear when his glider crashed. When he recovered consciousness he found everyone else inside the glider either dead or badly injured.

Some American Waco glider pilots met similar hazards. Pilot Wesley Hare and some of his passengers survived the impact of his glider diving straight into the ground when he lost control.

RAF glider pilot Rodney McEwan was guarding some German prisoners in a house when it came under attack from American paratroops. McEwan 'surrendered' to them.

Horsa pilot Tom Price, fighting on the ground, took prisoner four Germans who had simply walked up to him and surrendered.

Staff Sergeant Douglas Attwell arrived over the landing zone above the great pall of cloud, with gliders and powered aircraft being shot down. He landed on top of the Germans and could see the price being paid and the sacrifices made. The Germans were taking advantage of the easy targets presented by big gliders descending, and hundreds of gliders on the ground were being shot up by ground fire. Dead and wounded were everywhere. On the ground Dougie came across an abandoned pram, which he used to push a wounded man to an aid post.

At Earl's Colne Flight Sergeant Colin Peters sat in the Horsa's cockpit waiting for the take-off.

At 18 he had volunteered for the Royal Air Force, been selected for flying training and sent to South Africa, where he had gained his wings. On returning to England and expecting to be posted to Bomber Command, he had instead been seconded to The Glider Pilot Regiment, undergone a glider conversion course and was now about to take part in his first operation. As he looked out of the cockpit at the sunshine, he thought of his parents in the Rectory at Bridport and wondered whether he would see them again. Then Andy his co-pilot spoke and Colin's mind jerked back to the moment and the take-off procedure.

Airborne, he looked down at the wide spread of land below with the blue and green sea beyond. Over the water the shadows of the vast air-armada could be seen. Nearing the landing zone, flying through flak from 88-mm shells and automatics' bullets, the Horsa weaved, and below them the pilots could see numerous gliders, some wrecked, already on the ground. They also saw other gliders shot out of the sky. Inside the fuselage the Horsa's passengers sat ready, their weapons cocked for action. Touching down, the glider bumped and swung round, striking a tree sideways on. The impact tore the Horsa apart, its fuselage separated from the front section, leaving the pilots high and dry. Amazingly no one was injured and all went quickly into action.

Billy Wright, flying with his platoon of the 1st Royal Ulster Rifles in a glider, the pilot of which was named Walton, felt at first that all was going well and that he was foolish to have missed having any breakfast. But as the tug planes and gliders headed east across the Thames Estuary, he began to think of what lay ahead and wonder how he had become one of those sitting inside a flimsy aircraft with no engine. 'It was my first operation and I wondered about the landing and what sort of reception we would get. Would the Germans be waiting for us? Would we be attacked from the air, or the ground? Silently I said a small prayer. I remembered a quotation of Dr Johnson; he had said, "An appointment with the hangman concentrates the mind wonderfully". Certainly the thought of imminent death concentrated mine.

'However, once down, our glider pilot did a grand job, I was immediately involved in the unloading and then putting into action the tasks that my long training had prepared me for and all thoughts of fear, death and danger left my mind, concentrating on what my platoon leader expected me to do, and I suspect that was the case with all of us participating in the operation.'

Taking part in Operation Varsity, the Rhine crossing, Lieutenant Sidney St John was taken by surprise when arriving over the landing zone, he saw the dense smoke below him obscuring the ground. Halfway through his descent his glider entered the thick cloud and he was unable to see anything; then, to his alarm, when the Horsa emerged from the smoke he saw that he was very close to the ground, too close to make a proper landing, and the Horsa hit the soft ground at an angle, with automatic fire coming from all around. Everyone left the glider and took cover under a wing, while St John assessed the situation. His glider, a Mk. 1 type, had suffered some damage which caused the tail unit to jam to prevent the jeep inside being unloaded. However, with some explosive cord the problem was overcome.

Some time later, St John approached a house cautiously and suddenly came face to face with a middle-aged woman, who showed no surprise at seeing a British glider pilot. In fact, the Frau motioned him to enter the house and to sit at a table. Then she set some hot food before him. Relating the story, Sidney St John said, 'She did not appear to think of me being an enemy of her country and in fact fussed over me like a mother. When I ventured to the house I certainly did not expect to be provided with a hot meal by a German woman.'

Trevor Hathaway was 2nd pilot to Harry Deedes and after they had released from their tugplane both men were kept busy as they descended towards the landing zone. Then, at only 100 feet, machine guns opened up and Trevor was hit in both legs. Immediately, the Horsa touched down, the troops being carried inside it leapt out and quickly unloaded their equipment before dashing off towards their objective.

Meanwhile Harry Deedes lifted his co-pilot from the cockpit and onto the ground where, under a wing, he made Trevor as comfortable as possible before applying dressings to the wounds. Medics later found the wounded man and he was airlifted to a hospital near Swindon where thanks initially to the battlefield care of his pilot, he recovered.

Hamilcars in tow over the Rhine during operation 'Varsity'.

20

Misadventures

Luke Saunders served as a staff sergeant with both 'D' and 'N' Squadrons and he remembers a bizarre flying accident that only the luck of the order of flying saved him from being involved in.

L to R. Staff sergeants Luke Saunders, John Reardon, Jock Lowe and Joe Stonestreet.

'While at Number Three Glider Training school, Gaydon, training on Hotspurs towed by Miles Masters, navigation tests were carried out in Tiger Moths. In each aircraft two trainee-pilots participated. One, in the role of pilot sat in the rear seat and his companion, acting as a navigator, sat in the front cockpit, from which the 'stick' had been removed.

'One day, while the rest of the flight were occupied with their glider training, four of us were detailed to take the test. It was decided that the first pair should be Lieutenant A. Saunders as the pilot, and Corporal FitzGerald acting as navigator, while Corporal FitzPatrick and myself would await their return sixty minutes later and then make the test flight ourselves.

'Shortly before our take-off time we left the crew room to walk to the dispersal point and as we went we could see the rest of our flight busily engaged with their gliders in the distance. The Tiger Moth with Saunders and FitzGerald aboard was on its final approach and nearing touchdown when we saw it, then a very strong gust of wind caught it, blowing it off course and into a direct line with a clump of trees growing close to the end of the runway. The pilot pulled back his "stick" in an effort to lift the plane over the trees but it stalled and came down over our heads, and crashed on top of fuel storage tanks. The navigator was killed instantly and the pilot suffered considerable burns but survived.

'Corporal FitzPatrick and myself were ordered to return to the crew room and there learned that our test had been cancelled. Comrades returning later from their glider training had also seen the crash and believed that I had been in the plane. But for the Grace of God, I might have been.'

During the withdrawal that took place at the end of 'Market Garden', after nine days of bitter fighting and heroism, Lieutenant Ian Muir, RAMC, was positioned on the far bank of the Lower Rhine to tend wounded as they were helped ashore.

While watching boats carrying men draw nearer to the bank and men swimming, some of them drowning, he became aware of one soldier who was supporting himself on some unidentifiable flat object and forcing himself forward with powerful leg strokes. Reaching the bank and safety, the man dragged himself out of the water and pulled after him what the medical officer identified as a shield. 'It was decorated with the eagle and swastika of the Third Reich,' said the doctor, 'and I asked the soldier, a staff sergeant glider pilot, how he had come by it and he replied that he had "won" it from the Germans.'

'Unfortunately, I do not know the glider pilot's name, but he was unhurt and in excellent spirits as, with his trophy, he trudged off along the road towards the waiting transport.'

At an Elementary Flying Training School a trainee pilot, a lieutenant, progressed through all stages of the course with confidence and ease until he reached the time to make his first solo flight.

On the day, he climbed into the Tiger Moth with a cool assurance and settled comfortably, waiting for the signal to go. Then he taxied down the runway, gathering speed until the moment when the plane's wheels left the ground and he experienced the great thrill of knowing that he was airborne and flying on his own for the first time.

He made the usual circuit of the airfield and then began his approach and descent, everything going according to the book; he touched down and prepared to turn the plane and taxi towards where the instructor was waiting. Perhaps he was over-confident, or just careless, but whatever the reason he turned too sharply and too fast and the Tiger Moth's lower starboard wing touched the ground. The Tiger tilted alarmingly and it swung round through almost 180 degrees before the wheels settled again on the ground.

Regaining control, thc young pilot turned in the right direction, taxied to the required place, came to a halt and red-faced, got down from the cockpit, before slowly walking toward the instructor. He was probably expecting a rocket and perhaps the termination of his pilot training. However, his course record saved him and he went on to Glider Training School and achieved an excellent record of operational flying.

Staff Sergeant Arthur H. Mills' first operation was with the glider-borne invasion force that took off from North Africa in July 1943 to invade Sicily. But like many other glider pilots, he was forced to release the Waco he was piloting too far out to sea and unable to make a landfall, he pancaked the Waco on the water. Together with his co-pilot and the men of the South Staffordshire Regiment he was transporting, he spent five hours in the sea before being picked up by the SS *Ulster Monarch* and taken to Malta.

He returned to North Africa and later to Britain, where he was to take part in Operation Overlord. Unfortunately, having taken off from Keevil, piloting a Horsa to Normandy, he found the aircraft was nose-heavy and had to abort before reaching the English Channel.

But worse was to come. In September 1944, as part of the Arnhem invasion force for Operation Market Garden, he flew a Horsa to Holland, where he was subsequently wounded and taken prisoner. As a German prisoner of war he was confined in several Stalags and although still suffering from his wounds and weak from malnutrition, he was forced to endure a 400-mile march ahead of the advancing Russian army. Repatriated to England in 1945, he was found to be medically unfit and did not return to the regiment.

Staff Sergeants Douglas Jago and Gordon 'Dickie' Bird were close friends and had volunteered together for The Glider Pilot Regiment from the Royal Artillery.

Bird and his second pilot. Ron Cooper, were reported missing after flying their glider to Normandy on D-Day + 2 and his family received no further news of him. Doug Jago was taken prisoner at

Arnhem. Imagine his delighted surprise when, on arrival at Stalag Luft 1, one of the first men he saw was Dickie Bird standing by the wire to watch the arrival of the latest batch of 'Kriegies'.

John Moulton, formerly of the Essex Regiment, began his elementary flying training at Panshanger, Hertfordshire. One day he took off on his first solo cross-country flight. He was supremely confident and very happy that his training was going well. On the return leg of his course, however, the engine of his Tiger Moth began to misfire and he carefully nursed the plane towards the distant airfield. Eventually it became clear that the aircraft would not reach Panshanger and he began to look for somewhere to land. As he lost engine power he spotted a rough piece of ground behind a factory building which would have to suffice as an improvised landing strip. Carefully avoiding some parked vehicles, he managed to land safely. He was at Hatfield, just a short distance from the Panshanger airfield.

During a training flight pilot Victor Wade and his co-pilot Tony Jacob experienced the trauma of their towrope breaking and while Vic concentrated on flying the Horsa Tony gave his full attention to searching for somewhere suitable to make a safe emergency landing. The Horsa was losing height until, at only about 500 feet, Jago saw on their starboard a rectangular field surrounded by agricultural land and woodlands and told the pilot to make a 90° turn to line up the glider for its approach.

There was an 8 foot hedge along the approach boundary, the Horsa soared over it and touched down fast but almost immediately ran into an unseen ridge on the surface. The Horsa struck it hard causing it to bounce then just as it settled back and continued its run forward, it struck another ridge that proved to be its undoing. The glider stopped as though it had hit a wall and its tail lifted. The violence of the double impact caused the co-pilot's seat to collapse and Tony Jacob felt his hip dislocate!

Members of 87 Flt 'N' Squadron 1946. L to R S/Sgts. Jack Shaughnessy, Frank West, Jock Lowe, Alan Walker.

21

Victory in Europe

The rapid advance of the Allies led to the sudden end of war in Europe and a number of planned glider-borne landings being cancelled. On 30 April 1945 Adolf Hitler and his mistress, Eva Braun, committed suicide and four days later German generals surrendered unconditionally to General Montgomery, the British Supreme Commander.

Many glider-borne troops were not unhappy about the cessation of the use of gliders in Europe. For soldiers to be carried to battle behind enemy lines inside flimsy, uncomfortable and defenceless gliders was an experience not to be envied. Like glider pilots, the airborne troops were not issued with parachutes because until a glider landed it was impossible to get out. In flight pilots and their passengers faced the possibility of forced landings, should tow ropes break or tug-planes be shot down, or being peppered by shrapnel and bullets as the gliders descended, or of being unable to get out if a glider caught fire, or if its pilots were killed in the air. Then, as a glider approached its landing zone, there was always the possibility of a crash landing. Finally, after landing, before and during disembarking, there was the danger of attack from automatic weapons, rifles and mortars on the ground.

Despite their exploits, glider pilots, proud of their dual role as both pilots and total soldiers, did not enjoy the glamour of Royal Air Force pilots or paratroops in the eyes of the general public. Indeed, the paratroops have wrongly been credited with much of the success achieved by glider pilots. The *coup de main* successes at the River Orne and Caen Canal bridges have been attributed by a number of writers to the Parachute Regiment, even though the successes were achieved before paratroops arrived on the scene.

One glider pilot who took part in the London Victory Parade has said that he overheard a member of the public ask a companion, 'Who are those smart-looking men in maroon berets and wearing wings on their breasts?'

The recognition, early in the war, by Winston Churchill of the value of glider-borne troops and his determination to override all opposition from his generals and from the War Office, resulted in the formation of The Glider Pilot Regiment, but it was the drive, determination and enthusiasm of the Commander Glider Pilots, Brigadier George Chatterton, that brought about the *esprit de corps* of his pilots. They respected his style of leadership and his example of being able to do everything he asked of his men; that resulted in a regiment which, though short of tradition, earned an enviable reputation as a highly skilled fighting force, both in the air and on the ground. Every pilot was a first-class fighting man on the ground and able to fly several different types of aircraft. Each of them, too, had a great pride in the regiment and in themselves.

The Glider Pilot Regiment had proven its worth and in view of its effectiveness it was strange that the Germans failed to use gliders in large numbers. The Japanese too only used gliders in a very limited role, to carry supplies, not airborne troops.

Following upon the Allies' victory in Europe, the Supreme Commander, General D.W. Eisenhower, sent the following message, to be circulated and brought to the notice of all ranks:

SPECIAL ORDER OF THE DAY

Men and women of the Allied Expeditionary force. The Crusade has reached its glorious conclusion. It is my special privilege, in the name of all those Allied Nations represented in this theatre of war, to commend each and every one of you for your valiant performance of duty. Though these words are simple, they come from the bottom of a heart overflowing with pride for your loyal service, and admiration for you as warriors. Your accomplishments at sea, in the air, on the ground and in the field of supply, have astonished the world. Even before the final week of the conflict you had put five million of the enemy permanently out of the war. You have taken in your stride military tasks so difficult as to be classed, by many doubters, as being impossible. You have confused, defeated and destroyed your savagely fighting foe. On the road to Victory, you endured every discomfort and privation, surmounting every obstacle that the ingenious and desperate enemy could throw in your path. You did not pause until our front was firmly joined up with the great Red Army coming from the east, and other Allied forces from the south. FULL VICTORY IN EUROPE HAS BEEN ATTAINED. Working and fighting together, in a single and indestructible partnership, you have achieved a perfection of unification of air, ground and naval power that will stand as a model of our time.

The route you have travelled, through many hundreds of miles, is marked by the graves of fallen comrades. From them has been exacted the ultimate sacrifice. The life-blood of Allied Nations – American, British, Australian, Canadian, French, New Zealand, Polish and others – has helped us to gain Victory. Each of the fallen died as a member of the team to which you all belong, bound together by a common love of liberty and a refusal to submit to enslavement. No monument, no memorial, of whatever magnitude, can more aptly express our respect and veneration for their sacrifice, than will the perpetuation of the spirit of comradeship they shared with us who survive. As we celebrate Victory in Europe, let us remind ourselves that our common problems of the immediate and distant future can best be solved in the same spirit and devotion to the cause of human freedom that has made this Allied Expeditionary Force such a mighty engine of righteous destruction. Let us have no part in profitless quarrels, in which some men will undoubtedly engage, as to which country did most to win in the Europe War. Every man, every woman, every Nation represented among the Allies, have each contributed to victory. This we shall remember – and in doing so, we shall revere each honoured grave, and send comfort to those loved ones of our comrades who did not live to see this day.

(Signed) Dwight D. Eisenhower

As Eisenhower had noted, many of those, including glider pilots, who were instrumental in playing their part in the Allied victory had not survived to see it. Such is the nature of armed conflict. It is ironic that some of those who had survived the hostilities unscathed should fall victim to serious injury soon afterwards.

A few days after the armistice with Germany Rob McEvoy was posted to Fargo, Larkhill, from where he expected to be demobilised. Given a short leave, he went to the home of his sister and family at nearby Shrewton, a small village in rural Wiltshire and it was while there that he became the victim of a bizarre accident.

In those days milk was collected from farms in large churns which were left standing by the farmers on raised platforms beside the road, ready for dairymen to collect in their vans. One day, as McEvoy approached such a platform on his motorcycle, a dog which was sitting on it suddenly jumped down into the lane. The animal struck the motorcycle's front wheel, causing the rider to fall off and the bike landed on top of him. One of Rob's legs was so badly injured that it had to be amputated later.

22

Other Flying Activies

Following the end of the war in Europe, some glider pilots were posted to Burma, India, the Middle and Far East, while others were released to return to civilian life.

'N' Squadron Headquarters moved to the Regimental Depot at Fargo camp early in 1946 and at the end of that year Fargo was closed down. A small element of officers, NCOs and other ranks moved to Aldershot, where it became known as The Glider Pilot Depot Squadron, a part of the Airborne Forces Depot.

Volunteers were still being accepted into the regiment and after initial infantry training, they progressed to the Elementary Training Flying Schools (EFTS). The regiment was reduced to two operational squadrons, 'D' and 'N', with flying at Fairford, Netheravon, Oakington and Waterbeach, and courses for potential glider pilots at RAF Booker.

From Booker, after powered aircraft flying, potential glider pilots proceeded to Heavy Glider Conversion Units at Abingdon, North Luffenham and Upper Heyford, flying Horsa Mark II's. In 1948 'D' and 'N' Squadrons were redesignated 'A' and 'B' Squadrons.

During that time the regiment was involved, not for the first time, in experimental works, perfecting the 'snatching' technique of recovering gliders – an operation in which the tug aircraft flew over a parked glider at about 130 miles per hour and snatched it off the ground by means of a hooked steel cable housed in a steel channel. It was a method designed to recover undamaged gliders from battle areas.

Early in 1948 a flight of 'B' Squadron moved to North Germany as part of an Airborne Forces Group.

Glider flying had to be suspended during the Russian blockade of Berlin as the tug aircraft were kept busy, as were aircraft of the Royal Air Force, maintaining an airlift of vital supplies to the beleaguered German capital. Some glider pilots flew as second pilots with the RAF, and Staff Sergeant Joseph Toal was killed while acting in that role.

Those glider pilots stationed in Germany were returned to England in 1949 and glider training was briefly resumed until it was finally discontinued in 1950. Some of the pilots were then attached to each battalion of the 16th Parachute Brigade Group for field training and a number of others volunteered for parachute courses. As far as I am aware no member of the Parachute Regiment had ever volunteered to be flown in a glider!

In March 1951 an Army Council meeting decided to disband the regiment's one remaining squadron, and a decision was taken to train the pilots on Auster aircraft of the type flown by Royal Artillery pilots of the Air Observation Post (AOP). That training led to many of the regiment's pilots being posted to Malaysia, where their duties included flying over the jungles searching for the hideouts of terrorists. Two of the pilots, Staff Sergeant E.D. Gay and Staff Sergeant J. Perry, were killed during those operations.

23

Gliders in Burma

In the jungles of Burma General Orde Wingate was establishing a reputation as an unorthodox but highly successful commander. His policy was to penetrate deep behind the Japanese lines to cut their communications and supply lines. During March 1944 he began to use gliders with imagination and great success.

His technique was for the gliders – Waco CG-4As – to operate ahead of the army and to be landed in suitable clear patches in the jungle. The gliders carried bulldozers and other equipment suitable for clearing an airstrip and also mules for haulage purposes. As soon as an airstrip had been prepared, the troops and their military equipment were flown in by Dakotas, so establishing army units to operate as required behind the Japanese lines.

The gliders were towed by Dakotas, often in pairs and sometimes overloaded. Despite the fact that many of the operations were carried out at night, flying over very difficult country, the operations were remarkably successful. Almost 100 sorties were carried out, with the loss of 54 gliders, but well over 1,000 men, with their weapons and heavy equipment, were delivered safely to their objectives.

General Wingate was killed in an air crash in 1944, but the glider operations continued until May 1945.

24

Independent Squadrons in India

British pilots flying Hadrians and commanded by Major P. Stancliffe, had been sent to India in 1944 to form the nucleus of a glider force within a newly formed 44 Indian Airborne Division, which was part of South-East Asia Command (SEAC).

Initially there were 30 pilots, members of 10th Independent Squadron, and they were later increased in number to 143 by recruiting volunteers from army units in India and from Middle East Command,

Vice Admiral Lord Louis Mountbatten, Supreme Commander, SEAC, believed that the number of glider pilots needed should exceed 500 and wrote that their provision was a matter of urgency, which resulted in a meeting at Headquarters, Air Command, South-East Asia, where it was agreed that six squadrons, each of 80 Hadrians, would be formed and that the Hadrians would, later, be supplemented by Horsas and Hamilcars, with Halifaxes and Dakotas as tugs

To supplement the available Glider Pilot Regiment pilots, additional Royal Air Force pilots were attached as a temporary measure, but assured that they would remain RAF personnel. The army glider pilots were evenly distributed among the squadrons because of the benefit of their considerable experience and leadership,

Selection boards comprising experienced army glider pilots took place in Ambala, Jodhpur and Bequrnpet to interview volunteer glider pilots; those selected were promoted to sergeant and after qualifying received Second Glider Pilot Badges. By November the regiment had 13 squadrons and the glider pilots received training at a Jungle Survival School and at an RAF Mountain Centre. Additionally the NCOs underwent a platoon commanders' course to prepare them for the possible command of Indian troops should the latters' officers sustain casualties.

At the beginning of 1945, 24 glider pilots from 'E' and 'F' Squadrons, including two officers moved out to India from England.

In April a meeting at the Air Ministry was convened to consider the operational requirements of the airborne Forces for the remainder of the war in Europe and for operations elsewhere. At that time the impending end of the war with Germany was not known. Therefore it was decided to have sufficient pilots in the UK to fly 700 Horsas and 50 Hamilcars to transport any supplies sent to SEAC, where the requirement was for 4,000 Wacos and 540 Horsas. For the future, gliders would be required in Thailand and Sumatra.

JAPAN

On 6 August 1945, a United States B-29 bomber took off from a small island in the Pacific Ocean, heading towards Japan. On board with the six-man crew was a uranium bomb. Shortly after 0800 hours it reached Hiroshima and the bombardier released the bomb. It exploded high above the ground.

Later the pilot described what he saw: 'We felt the heat from the flash and the concussion from the blast . . . there was a mushroom-like expanse of dust and then the centre plumed up to a great height and a huge dustcloud spread all over the city.'

More than 70,000 Japanese died instantly and it was estimated that some 200,000 more died later from the effects of radiation.

Three days later the Americans dropped another on Nagasaki, with the same devastating effects. The result of those two bombs was horrific but countless Allied lives – including those of British prisoners of war held in appalling conditions in prison camps in Burma, Thailand and Singapore – were saved.

After nearly six years of war, the news that Japan had surrendered unconditionally was broadcast at midnight on 14 August 1945. The threat to our freedom and the restrictions of our existence, suddenly evaporated and uppermost in the minds of men and women on active service and their loved ones at home was a determination to make the most of our freedom and to build a new future so that succeeding generations would never be confronted with such an ordeal again.

Sadly, though, the world was never again to know peace of mind. The Atomic Age had arrived, with the worry that some-one's finger, somewhere, might be hovering around the button.

Where did we go wrong?

25

The Holy Land – Palestine, 1945–1948

With the end of the war in Europe Jews began clamouring to be allowed to go to Palestine, as Israel was then called. The survivors of Hitler's death camps and other anti-Semitic horrors set their hearts on going to live in the Promised Land and once again the British made every effort to help, providing shipping to Palestine and assistance with housing, albeit with a limit on the numbers each year. Many Jews felt that the British Government should allow unlimited numbers to travel and saw its refusal to increase the annual number as an affront to both Jewish ambitions and to justice. This led to conflict with the nation that had been both their champion and saviour.

Many glider pilots and other troops were at that time looking forward to the date of release from the service, but when 6th Airborne Division, made up of three brigades of paratroops and an element of The Glider Pilot Regiment, was ordered to Palestine as part of the Middle East Strategic Reserve, many who were hoping for an early demobilisation were sent to the Middle East.

I was one of several glider pilots who set sail from Southampton aboard the SS *Carnarvon Castle*. We had been told that we would join a flight of 'G' Squadron in Egypt. However, after landing at Alexandria and travelling overland to GHQ Cairo, we were told that the element of 'G' Squadron was no longer in Egypt, all pilots and gliders having been sent to India. We were then despatched to a tented camp beside the Suez Canal, at Ismailia.

After making a number of visits to Cairo, where I was persistent in my inquiries about The Glider Pilot Regiment, I was posted to Palestine, in the rank of major, to be second in command of the 2nd Mechanised Regiment and travelled overnight across the Sinai Desert to take up my appointment.

As dawn broke I saw citrus plantations, twisted olive trees growing on terraces, bright yellow mimosa blossoms and ancient buildings. The visual appeal of the Holy Land was immense. However, with no opportunities of flying, life was somewhat tedious. Our role was one of diplomacy allied to an alertness against any hostile action by some of the Jews and also to thwart the stealth and cunning of some of the Arabs, who could steal anything, even from within guarded camps.

The Jews then in Palestine were of two types: those who for years had lived in harmony with the Palestinian Arabs and the newcomers from war-torn Europe with a growing hatred for Britain and the British. To achieve their demands for unlimited immigration into Palestine they embarked on a campaign of hostility against both the British and the Palestinian Arabs.

British troops were under instructions to act as peacemakers, a very difficult role when being provoked. Three main underground organisations sprang up from among the Jews; the first, the Haganah, was a national army of men and women who were well-equipped with arms but were more moderate than the other organisations. The other two, the Irgun Zvai Leumi and the Stern Gang, were more extremist and attracted the more hot-headed younger Jews of both sexes. They perpetrated atrocities on both Arabs and British soldiers, with the intention of preventing an Arab–Jewish partition of the Holy Land and the rights of the indigenous Arabs were ignored.

With the recall of my commanding officer to an appointment in London, I assumed acting command of the 2nd Mechanised Regiment. When Field Marshal Sir Alan Brooke, later Lord Alanbrooke, visited the troops in the Middle East he invited me to accompany him to Jordan, Syria and Lebanon in the role of acting ADC. On rejoining my regiment in Hebron I found life less than exciting, but I did have some pleasant interludes.

At Christmas, unusually for Palestine, snow fell and I took the opportunity to visit Bethlehem. Tourism was then unknown and the ancient city appeared unchanged since Biblical times. Around the square were chalk-coloured buildings, including a mosque and a Christian church said to have been built over the site of Jesus Christ's birthplace. In a semi-basement chamber is the place where the infant Jesus is said to have been born. Early in my time in the Holy Land I learned that 'G' Squadron of The Glider Pilot regiment was stationed near Tel Aviv and went there. I was told that the flight I had expected to join in Egypt had not gone to India, but were in fact not far from where I had spent those boring weeks at Ismailia.

On another occasion I was a guest at a banquet given by King Abdullah of Jordan, in Amman. Inside the palace entrance a row of distorting mirrors lined a wall and the King stood on the stairs chortling at the distorted reflections of his guests.

My adrenalin-charged flying days, when I flew both powered aircraft and gliders, were behind me and my days were instead occupied with impressing upon my officers and men that they must at all times exercise restraint, despite many terrorist-inspired occasions when groups of men and women would taunt my men in an effort to provoke them into taking retaliatory action. Rail tracks and rolling stock and aeroplanes on the ground were blown up. Then came an appalling daylight abduction on a Jerusalem street of three off-duty sergeants. Their bodies were subsequently found hanging in a eucalyptus grove.

On a later occasion a bomb was planted in a part of the King David Hotel, Jerusalem, that was used as British Middle East Command Headquarters. The resultant explosion killed and injured almost 100 men and women.

One day, while being driven from Jerusalem down the steeply winding road to the Dead Sea some 1,000 feet below sea level, I myself became a casualty when my car was ambushed near where the Bible says the Good Samaritan lived. The road runs between high rocky slopes on one side and a deep valley on the other. My companions were killed and I, wounded, was pushed over the side of the road into the deep ravine. Fortunately an overhanging bush saved me and my body lay, badly injured, until seen from below by an Arab shepherd who summoned help. After many operations and much care from surgeon Captain Ian Sutherland, my limbs were saved from amputations, and in August 1949 I was discharged from both hospital and the army, 100 per cent disabled, ten years after I enlisted 'for the duration'. Those young men who joined the forces at the same time as myself and who had survived, had been back in 'Civvie Street' for several years. (My disability was subsequently reduced to a permanent 80 per cent.)

Peter Cotton was surprised to be posted to Palestine so near to his anticipated release date and, like many of the glider pilots he sailed with, he had been counting the months to his anticipated release date and the resumption of his civilian occupation in a bank. However, like the others, he resigned himself to making the most of what he foresaw as a quiet life in an interesting country.

The realisation was very different. His flying days were suddenly behind him and instead he had to endure a restrictive non-aggressive role as a peacemaker. The hostility of many of the Jews had to be borne without retaliation and many times Pete gritted his teeth as he strove to subdue a natural feeling of anger. 'Why', he thought, 'have Jews, the oppression of whom by the Nazis had led us into six years of war, suddenly turned against us? There was a mobile radio station that, several times a day, always at the same times, broadcast anti-British propaganda. After each broadcast it moved somewhere else, which made it very difficult to find. Eventually though, it was located and the equipment destroyed. Despite the restrictions placed upon us when suffering verbal abuse and our policy of non-retaliation, the Holy Land proved to be a most fascinating and interesting country.'

Donald Coppin arrived in Sarafand with other glider pilots early in 1946, after sailing in SS *Strathnaver* to Port Said and then travelling overland into Palestine. For him too the adrenalin-filled days of flying were oft-remembered as he fulfilled the daily non-aggressive and peacekeeping role of 6th Airborne Division. One memory of that time that remains with him was of an occasion shortly before Christmas 1946 when General Montgomery visited Sarafand and talked to officers inside a cinema. Don was posted to the roof of the building to act as a guard in case of any hostile action from one of the underground movements and he remembers feeling very exposed and vulnerable. The occasion, however, proved to be uneventful.

Staff Sergeant Roy Farren, stationed with glider pilots at Sarafand, Palestine, was in Jerusalem, where he unexpectedly met a friend from his native Gloucester. She was a commissioned nursing sister at the British Military Hospital and during their time together she suggested that she would take him to see something that was not on view generally and which he might consider to be both unusual and in the worst taste.

'She was proved to be right,' said Roy, 'and on our way to the hospital she said that the building had formerly been a German embassy, or similar. On arrival she took me to the chapel within the main building. Behind the altar was a very large colourfully painted mural that stretched almost wall-to-wall. It depicted the Last Supper, but what astounded me was that the face of the figure sitting with his disciples was not that of Jesus Christ, but instead was that of Kaiser Wilhelm, the former German Emperor who had led the German nation into the bloodiest war of all time, World War I, 1914 to 18.

'It was both bizarre and blasphemous and I have often wondered since what was the mural's ultimate fate. I heard much later that the hospital had been taken over by the Israel Government and used as a university.'

Sergeant Keith Miller in front of a Hamilcar.

The author in 1945.

26

Exeunt

In 1947 the United Nations agreed that there should be a partition of Palestine to create separate Jewish and Arab states, the prime and Jewish section to be called Israel, the new Jewish Promised Land.

The Glider Pilot Regiment left during the second half of 1947 but the flight in Egypt remained there until early 1948 before returning to England.

In England the rundown of the regiment was taking effect, with glider stations closing, followed by the closure of the Regimental Depot at Fargo, Salisbury Plain and with a smaller headquarters, comprising three officers and eighteen others, being set up at Aldershot, to become part of the Airborne Forces Depot. The headquarters members still performed their normal role, receiving volunteers, sending them for infantry training and then posting them to Elementary Flying Training School (EFTS).

Brigadier Chatterton had retired midway through 1945 and The Glider Pilot Regiment's new Commander was Lieutenant Colonel C.J. Deedes, MC. In April 1948, a flight of Horsas was posted to RAF Schleswigland in Germany. On New Year's Day 1949 glider pilots went to RAF Wunstorf, Germany, and flew as co-pilots with the RAF on York aircraft flying in and out of Berlin during the airlift of that year.

In 1950 there were alterations to the regiment's insignia when an

Army Order designated 'The Glider Pilot and Parachute Corps' with effect from 22 May 1950. The Army Air Corps was disbanded from that date, which led to the initials AAC and laurel wreath on the regiment's cap badge being replaced by a scroll bearing the regiment's name. It was a dramatic change for, since February 1942, the Army Air Corps had embraced first The Glider Pilot Regiment, followed by the Parachute Regiment when it was formed later in the year and the Special Air Service from 1944. The two latter eventually adopted their individual badges, but The Glider Pilot Regiment returned to the 'AAC' one. At the same time, the regiment adopted an arm badge in the form of a Horsa in flight.

The final flights of troop-carrying gliders were made in 1950.

On 9 December 1950 a fine stained-glass memorial window was unveiled in Salisbury Cathedral by Field Marshal Lord Alanbrooke, KG, GCB, OM, GCVO, DSO, the Colonel Commandant, to the honour and glory of God and to those 553 pilots of the regiment who gave their lives during 1942–45. In 1951 it was confirmed that in future gliders would not take part in airborne operations and that to maintain a nucleus of pilots 'Light Liaison Flights' would be set up, to be attached to Air Observation Post (AOP) squadrons to provide a reserve of pilots. AOP squadrons operated with the Royal Artillery, the pilots accurately assessing the effects of artillery fire, finding enemy targets and ranging RA guns on to them.

AOP squadrons operated during the Korean War and elsewhere.

Army flying continues today at Middle Wallop, Hampshire, by the Army Air Corps, which was founded in 1957. The War Office refused it permission to adopt the former Glider Pilot Regiment's maroon beret, so its personnel wear a light blue beret with The Glider Pilot Regiment's 'eagle' cap badge.

The very fine Museum of Army Flying, with its many Glider Pilot Regiment exhibits, is also sited at Middle Wallop, Hants.

The regiment was perhaps the smallest and most short-lived of the regiments of the British Army but it enjoyed a unique role and an *esprit de corps* that is unsurpassed. All who served with it enjoyed the comradeship of a regiment ranking high in the history of the British army and epitomising Brigadier George Chatterton's desire for *total soldiers*.

One thing that was proved with the use of gliders was that they had an advantage over paratroops in that they could deliver a compact force of troops and their weapons and equipment directly on target and ready for action. A stick of paratroops upon landing was spread out over a wide area, making them vulnerable to attack until able to get together as a fighting force.

Gliders though, were highly vulnerable from attack in the air and from ground defences. They were large, slow and unarmed. As a means of defence many operations were carried out at night, but night flying required a higher standard of training than it was practical to give glider pilots as the length of the war extended. Subsequent daylight operations were successful, providing that the element of surprise was maintained.

At the same time gliders were expensive to build and many of them were damaged or smashed up as a result of crash landings in enemy territory. (Major Peter Jackson, who was among the first to join The Glider Pilot Regiment, was involved in some retrieving operations of undamaged gliders.)

The gliders' strength was gradually run down after the end of World War II and the Army Air Corps now uses helicopters which are capable of flying back to their home airfield after delivering their loads and can be kept in continuous operation.

27

Tributes to Glider Pilots

Padre Eric Davies was flown to battle areas by gliders. In a letter written from Singapore, he paid the following tribute:

'I got used to flying as a passenger in gliders and had an excellent rapport with the glider pilots and the glider-borne troops. Some were, at first, a bit inhibited about travelling with a padre in such confined space but I soon became accepted as a friend with whom they could share a laugh, discuss worries and confide family and personal problems. Even the most anti-religious among them came round to doing so. Indeed I never met an atheist on any field of battle.

'Among so many patriotic and brave young men none surpassed the glider pilots. They embodied the spirit of The Glider Pilot Regiment as both skilled pilots and superb and versatile fighting men on the ground. On many occasions I saw glider pilots giving calm assurance to the men they flew to battle areas. I witnessed them handling many and varied types of weapons and they were men who were capable of immediately taking command of any situation, quietly and efficiently. Their very high level of airmanship, courage and discipline justified the demands of their Commander, Colonel George Chatterton and raised the standard of The Glider Pilot Regiment to the highest degree of efficiency and respect.

'Although the Regiment was small in numbers and was in being for only a few years, its reputation will be noted in military history as having earned the right to battle honours and to be listed among the finest fighting regiments of all time.

'The inclusion of a fine stained-glass window in Salisbury Cathedral to commemorate those glider pilots who gave their lives, can also be seen as a tribute to all glider pilots; airmen-soldiers who earned the respect of both allies and enemies.'

Perhaps the best of many accolades to the pilots who flew with The Glider Pilot Regiment was expressed by General Guyman of the United States airborne forces. He wrote:

> 'British glider pilots were the most uninhibited individuals in the fighting forces of any nation.
> Flying fragile, unpowered aircraft, without parachutes, on assaults deep into enemy-held territory and having a special military skill as combatants on the ground, they were unsurpassed throughout World War II.'

The *News Chronicle*'s leading article on 8 December 1944 included the following appreciation of The Glider Pilot Regiment:

> While most of the famous British Regiments have many hundreds of years of tradition, The Glider Pilot Regiment, formed only in the early days of this War, has won glory from its earliest days. Their first major action was in Sicily, then came the highly successful *coup de main* at the Caen Canal and River Orne bridges, hours in advance of the Parachute Regiment and the Allied invasion forces, followed by successful landings and actions in Normandy and the tough episodes of Arnhem and the Rhine Crossing.

EPILOGUE

The *Daily Telegraph* carried the following reports:

(19 April 1945)

VICTIMS STACKED IN HEAPS AT BELSEN

> The Senior Medical Officer of the Second Army has been for forty eight hours at the German concentration camp at Belsen, which was liberated three days ago by General Dempsey's British troops. The Brigadier said it was 'the most horrible frightful place' he had ever seen.
>
> He described how he found 40,000 half-dead prisoners, corpses in great heaps and thousands of cases of typhus, typhoid and tuberculosis.
>
> His revelations followed upon those made on the liberation of two other concentration camps at Nordhausen and Buchenwald.
>
> 'I am told,' he said, 'that 30,000 prisoners died during the last few months and can well believe that figure.'
>
> Here is his description of what he saw and of the steps taken to alleviate the suffering of those still alive.
>
> The unclothed bodies of women formed a great pile sixty metres long, thirty metres wide and two metres high, within the sight of children.

Gutters were filled with dead. Men had gone to the gutters to die.

There was bunk accommodation for only 474 of the 1,704 women suffering from acute typhus, typhoid and tuberculosis. An additional 18,600 women who should have been in hospital were lying on bare bug-ridden boards.

In the men's quarters there were 1,900 bunks for 2,242 acute cases of illness and another 7,000 men should have been in hospital.

'The prison doctors tell me that cannibalism had been going on,' the Brigadier said, 'There was no flesh on the emaciated bodies, and livers, kidneys and hearts were cut out.'

The *Daily Telegraph* leader said:

Nazi concentration camps have always been a synonym for horrors, but the worst ever reported, or imagined thing about them is far outweighed by the realities being discovered daily by the Allied troops as one ghastly charnel heap after another of naked men, women and children's bodies awaiting cremation, or the emaciated forms of the half-dead racked with disease, filth, hunger and hopeless misery are found. The subjects of organised mass-murder by starvation, by unbelievable tortures and by deliberate overcrowding in hovels unfit for human habitation. Their 'guards', all of them Himmler's men; betrayed more than an utterly callous indifference to their suffering; prisoners who tried to pilfer food from the swill bins were, if seen, shot. The most merciless of medieval torturers would have shrunk in horror at what was enacted in the twentieth century in the heart of a country that has been professing to hold something like a monopoly of 'culture'.

The Allied High Command is taking praiseworthy steps to see

that those responsible for such appalling treatment are suitably punished and to that end are ensuring that the eye-witnesses of German concentration camps include enough German citizens to refute any claims, during trials, that stories are untrue, or exaggerated. A thousand Weimar citizens of both sexes, for example, have made an enforced tour of inspection at Buchenwald and that is a method which should be repeated at every camp. Responsibility for the barbarities practised through the years rest with the whole German people, who were ready enough to applaud Hitler and his gangsters in the heyday of success.

That responsibility cannot be expiated merely by defeat. The facts now brought to light will redouble the determination of the United Nations that every identifiable executant of these crimes shall be condemned and punished with the utmost rigour of law.

(30 April 1945)

MUSSOLINI EXECUTED BY PATRIOTS

British War correspondents who entered Milan yesterday saw the bodies of Mussolini, Clara Petacci and 16 of his henchmen being publicly exhibited in a square in the city, it was officially announced in an Allied HQ statement last night.

Mussolini and his Fascist leaders were reported earlier by Italian partisan-controlled radios to have been executed by Italian patriots after a brief trial by a people's tribunal.

Those who died with Mussolini – the executions took place on Saturday afternoon – include his mistress Clara Petacci, Carlo Scorza and Alessandro Pavolini, former secretary-general of the Fascist party and Francesco Baraccu, Vice-President of the Council of Ministers.

The war correspondents said that Mussolini and the others were seized in Como while trying to escape to Switzerland.

They said that Mussolini and the other Fascists were executed at 4.20 p.m. on Saturday, in the town of Guliano di Mezzegere, near Como. The bodies were then taken by truck to Milan for public display in the same square where 15 patriots had been executed by the Fascists.

An Allied Forces HQ announcement said that the reporters had personally seen the bodies of Benito Mussolini, the Italian Fascist dictator and the others lying in the Piazza Loretto, where the populace filed past to view the corpses and revile them.

Large crowds also flocked from the surrounding countryside into Milan yesterday to see the bodies hanging, according to the Italian resistance radio.

Allied tanks entering Milan were stopped by the sight of the bodies of Mussolini and the others hanging at a petrol pump station in a Milan square.

One woman was seen to fire 5 shots into the already bullet-ridden body of Mussolini, crying 'Five shots for my five assassinated sons'.

(1 May 1945)

HITLER COMMITS SUICIDE IN THE FACE OF DEFEAT

The death was announced over the German radio, of Adolf Hitler, last night. The statement said that it took place at his command post in Berlin, now almost completely occupied by Russian troops. The text of the announcement was:

'It is reported from the Fuehrer's HQ that our Fuehrer, Adolf

Hitler, has fallen this afternoon at his command post in the Reich Chancellery, fighting to the last breath against Bolshevism and for Germany. On Monday the Fuehrer appointed Grand Admiral Doenitz as his successor.

The thin-lipped Admiral, who has made the study of submarines his life's work, has always hated Britain. He was an officer in the German navy during World War I and volunteered for U-boat service and was attacked by a British ship, depth-charged and when Doenitz brought her to the surface he and his crew were taken prisoners.

He was later certified insane and transferred to Manchester Lunatic-Asylum from his prisoner-of-war camp. In 1919 he was repatriated as insane.'

(15 August 1945)

JAPAN UNCONDITIONAL SURRENDER

Japan has surrendered unconditionally. This was announced simultaneously at midnight in London, Washington and Moscow by Clement Attlee, President Truman and in a State broadcast by Moscow radio.

General MacArthur has been appointed Supreme Commander to receive the Japanese surrender and Britain, Russia and China will be represented by high-ranking officers.

In the meantime, Allied forces have been ordered to suspend offensive action.

In Britain victory holidays will be today and tomorrow. HM the King will broadcast at nine p.m. this evening.

Mr Attlee and President Truman both read the Japanese reply to the Allies surrender terms. The reply was received through the Swiss Minister in Washington last night. President Truman said it was 'a full acceptance of the Potsdam declaration, which specifies the unconditional surrender of Japan.'

The Emperor of Japan was due to broadcast to his people at midnight.

(15 August 1945)

THE END

Final and total surrender by the last of our enemies. That is the message which Prime Minister Clement Attlee was able to give to the country at midnight.

Peace descends upon the world again after six years, within three weeks, of war which has devastated civilisation on a scale never seen before.

Recovery will take many a year, but the carnage has ceased and the nations are free to turn to the tasks of reconstruction with such speed as concentrated resolution may wring from the material impoverishment that is the aftermath of war. In the hour of triumph solemn resolves will mingle with the joy of a public holiday and resolves to apply every resource to overtake the heavy tasks which lie before us and determination that no aggressor shall be allowed to provoke such a conflict again.

PHOTOGRAPHS

My grateful thanks to

George Burn

John Concannon

Ronald Hobbs

Roy Howard

Keith J Miller

Luke Saunders

Gordon Swansborough

Victor Wade

for their help in illustrating this book and to George Burn for his drawings of gliders.

BIBLIOGRAPHY

My research for this book has been principally achieved through the medium of personal interviews, conversations and correspondence with people who were involved in the various operations of the Glider Pilot Regiment, members of other airborne forces, or those who had tenuous connections with them and included reading contemporary newspaper reports.

I have however, also gained valuable assistance from the following publications:

Chatterton, George, *The Wings of Pegasus*, London, Macdonald, 1962

Smith, Claude, *The History of The Glider Pilot Regiment*, London, Leo Cooper, 1992

Lloyd, Alan, *The Gliders*, London, Leo Cooper, 1982

I have also contacted some members of the regimental association who had contributed to the regimental journal *The Eagle*, of which I was a former editor, to obtain permission to quote from them.

Every attempt has been made to trace copyright holders of material and the author apologises for any omissions.

INDEX